On
Summer

*And Other Simple
Stories of Faith and Family*

Life Is Swift As A
Sunset And Short
As An Autumn Day

KEN PIERPONT

For more information on
Ken Pierpont's writing and ministry go to:
KenPierpont.com

DEDICATION

Dedicated to my merciful Lord Jesus Christ;
to my patient, loyal family;
and to my parents:
Kenneth Frederick Pierpont
Jane Ann Pierpont

CONTENTS

INTRODUCTION

In a small town in southeastern Ohio, seventy years ago a little boy lay in his bed at night paralyzed with fear. He was sure there was a stranger in the dark corner of his room. His mother was in the next room of their simple cottage home listening to the radio. He called out to her in fear. When she parted the curtain that served as the door to his bedroom he could see that the dark form in the corner was not an intruder, but his father's hunting coat.

She said, "What do you need?"

Embarrassed, he answered, "Could you pray with me?"

"Go ahead," she said, sitting down on the edge of the bed.

Now I lay me down to sleep.
I pray the Lord my soul to keep.
If I should die before I wake,
I pray the Lord my soul to take.

"That's nice; now go to sleep," his mother said with a touch of impatience in her voice as she rose to leave.

Just as she reached the doorway the little boy called, "Mom, what happens when you die?" She turned back and answered softly, "I don't know; now go to sleep," and then she left the room. But the question didn't go away. Even though he regularly attended church growing up, it was years later when someone finally helped him find the answer to the question, "What happens when you die?" The answer changed his life forever.

In Michigan there lived a little girl whose parents' divorce plunged her into pain and confusion. On August 28, 1948, a large tent was erected down the street from her house. She thought it was a circus. She and her sister went to investigate. The tent had been erected by a church to hold a summer Vacation Bible School. It was there she heard the story of Jesus for the first time. She was young, but she knew the burden of guilt. She was a sinner. She understood that Jesus died for her and that she could be forgiven and have eternal life through faith in Christ alone. Eventually her parents would both find Christ and reunite their family under new management.

The little boy carried his question in his heart unanswered into his early twenties. Then, as a young sailor away from home, his spiritual quest came to an end and a beginning. Buddies from the Navy challenged him to turn his empty religion into life-altering faith. After his grandmother's funeral he found a book by Billy Graham and read it on a late-night bus ride back to Great Lakes

Naval Air Station near Chicago. His questions, his grief, his guilt, and his friends' witness converged to draw him over the threshold of faith into the family of God.

At a church picnic a few months later, that young lady and that young man met. On Christmas Eve 1955 they started out together determined to build a Christian family and a Christian home. All the stories in this book spring from that story—the story of how my mother and father were changed forever by the story of Jesus, the Gospel.

This is a book of stories—true, simple stories of my family, our lives, and our faith. They are not the whole story, just a few snapshots and video clips about people I know and love and things that I have observed. Like all stories, they are rooted in the stories that go before them and affect the stories that follow them. And there is a greater story, a story that includes every human being who has ever lived and will include all who are to come. It is my prayer that the stories I share here will help you see your place in the romance, the adventure, the mystery, the tragedy, the comedy, the overarching story of the ages.

I hope, whoever you are, that reading these stories will help you be as happy as it is humanly possible to be in this life and the next.

–Ken Pierpont

KEN PIERPONT

Chapter 1
A WRINKLE IN MY HOOD

We live in a very quiet neighborhood. Late one evening I was listening to some music when I heard a loud crash on the street. It took me a while to realize what had happened.

Earlier that evening my wife had wanted me to go to the store to get some soft drinks. It seemed like a good time to let my teenage daughter get in a little practice driving. I sent her to the store with her older brother riding shotgun. She took my truck. I settled back to enjoy the music.

At dinner earlier that evening my oldest son was speaking admiringly of the truck. It is a little four-wheel drive Ford Explorer, and the kids know I have enjoyed having it. It is the nicest car I have ever owned.

I said, "Guys, my heart is not set on that car. I like it, but it is just rusting metal and it is a depreciating item. It won't last forever. Never set your heart on anything temporary."

I had no idea how prophetic my advice was that night.

The thud on the street was followed by a commotion upstairs and then the whole family pouring down the steps, led by thirteen-year-old Chuck, who shouted, "Dad, Dad, Holly wrecked your car!"

My heart sank and my mind was flooded with conflicting thoughts. Was anyone hurt? Who else was involved? I ran to the door with a racing heart and in that instant a message came clearly to my spirit like a voice in my heart: "Here is your chance. You have always looked for ways to show Holly that she is precious to you. Here is a unique opportunity to show her what you really love. How you react now is something that she will probably never forget."

To my surprise the accident had not occurred on the street, but right in my own driveway. And my fears about damage to the property of other people melted when I saw that the collision was with our other car, the family van. In her inexperience Holly had stepped on the accelerator when she meant to step on the brakes. In an instant both of my cars were wrecked. Holly was unhurt physically but when I reached her she was crying softly and saying over and over again, "Oh, Dad, I'm sorry. I'm sorry, Dad. I know how much you love this car." I wrapped her in my arms and she cried and my heart melted for her.

Later that week a friend stopped by and asked what had happened to my truck. I swore her to secrecy and then told her what had happened. Her eyes moistened and she said, "That happened to me when I was a girl. I borrowed my dad's car and ran into a log that had fallen across the road. I was able to drive the car home, but it was totaled. When I got home my dad dragged me from the car, knocked me to the ground, and began to kick me." Over forty years later the pain of that rejection still moved her to tears. It was a deep wound on her soul.

I remembered how tenderhearted Holly had been the night she wrecked the car and how vulnerable she was at that moment, and I breathed a prayer of thanks to God for his gentle reminder that night. Someday years from now when Holly thinks back on her life and she remembers me, I want her to know that I loved her a thousand times more than all my earthly possessions put together.

I repaired the van, but the wrinkle in the hood of my truck is still there today. Every day it reminds me of the really priceless things in my life. I don't mind having damage to my truck, but I don't want to be responsible for damage to my daughter's heart.

Chapter 2
THE FATHER'S VOICE

Sometimes you can be enjoying a beautiful, mundane afternoon and be plunged into a heartrending crisis within a few seconds. That happened to us one quiet spring afternoon a few years ago. I was walking out across the yard enjoying the laughter and play-sounds of the children coming from the other side of the barn.

There was an old corncrib beyond the barn, and the children loved to pretend it was a jail. It was made of wire and rusty angle iron and had a door with a latch.

A few times in my life I have had impressions, strong mystical inner feelings. Sometimes they prompt me to fulfill some obligation; sometimes they are like sweet whispered promises from the Lord; sometimes they warn of danger. Walking toward the barn I had a strong impression in my heart to call for little Heidi. All the children were playing there beyond the barn and out of sight, but it was Heidi who came to my mind. There was a feeling of urgency attached to the thought.

"Heidi," I called. "Come here." Nothing.

"Heidi." No answer.

I felt a stirring feeling in my heart and called out again, louder this time, wishing she would answer.

"Heidi."

What I saw next is a scene that I will never forget. Heidi is a beautiful little girl. She has long blonde hair and blue eyes the color of a mountain lake. Her voice is low like her mother's and sisters' voices. She is a quiet middle child who has always been easy to raise.

She came through the barn door, out from the shadows of the barn and into the sunlight, and her beautiful little face was covered with blood from a gash on her forehead. It made my heart hurt to see it. It still hurts to think about it.

The children spilled out the details of the story. One of the children was in the "jail" and trying to get out. A small stick was in the latch. He knew if he kicked the door the stick would snap and he would be free. He kicked with all his might at the same moment Heidi walked in front of the door. The sharp frame of angle iron caught her in the center of her forehead.

The children crowded around her with fearful looks on their faces. It was clear this was not going to be a do-it-yourself first-aid job. She was heading for the emergency room for stitches. Immediately I began to feel sick about the scar that would most certainly mar her pretty little face.

I would so willingly have traded places with her. Lois and I cleaned her up and Lois used a butterfly bandage to close the wound until I could get her to the doctor. It was about twenty miles to his office. The office was closed, but he agreed to meet us there anyway.

All the way, the lump stayed in my throat and my heart raced. I prayed, "O Lord, please don't let Heidi's pretty little face have a scar."

When we finally arrived at the doctor's office, he said, looking at the butterfly bandage, "Who did this?"

"Her mother," I said.

"I'm not going to touch this," he said. "This will heal up fine the way it is. You tell your wife she did a great job."

I reached for my wallet. The doctor stopped me. "Listen, you don't owe me anything. Just see to it this little girl gets some ice cream on the way home."

"Will there be a scar?" I asked.

"Ken, in a few weeks I doubt if you will even remember this happened," he said reassuringly.

I thanked the good man and warmly shook his hand. Heidi and I walked to the car. Little Heidi's hand was in mine. Back in the car my heart settled and a wave of thanksgiving and relief flooded over me. I breathed a prayer of thanksgiving to the Lord, and then Heidi and I thanked the Lord together.

We headed to Dairy Queen. The doctor usually

charges about $60 a visit, so I figured with $30 apiece we could really tank up.

We ate our ice cream and drove along together in quietness.

"Heidi," I asked as we drove, "did you hear me calling you, Sweetheart?"

"Yes," she answered quietly in her little low voice.

"Did you come the first time you heard me call?"

"No."

"Why, Honey?"

"I was going to come, but I just wanted to go over to the corncrib first." "Is that when you got hurt?"

"Yes."

"Oh, Heidi," I said. "Do you realize if you would have come the first time you were called you would never have been hurt? God told me to call you before you got hurt."

The road wound home over green hills covered with the tender grass of early spring. We drove slowly, enjoying our time together. My grateful heart meditated upward toward my Heavenly Father. I wonder how many painful mistakes I could have avoided in my life if I had come the first time my Father called.

"Every good gift and every perfect gift is from above, and comes down from the Father of lights, with whom there is no variation or shadow of turning" (James 1:17).

". . . No good thing will He withhold from those who walk uprightly" (Psalm 84:11).

Chapter 3
ROADKILL

When I was a boy we lived in a wide spot in the road called Logansville. My dad was the parson of the Congregational Church there. Friday was payday, and in good weather I rode my bike up the hill west of town to Huber Rhorer's house to pick up Dad's check. It was eighty dollars a week. Friday nights we all went to town.

Going to town on Friday nights in our family was a dress-up occasion. No Levi's or sneakers were allowed.

The whole family would walk though the grocery store while Mom and Dad picked out our week's worth of groceries. If there was a little extra we would go to Clancey's hamburger stand and get the works: hamburger, small fries, and a soft drink. In the summer we would often stop for a small vanilla cone. If we needed clothes and had the money we would usually shop at the United store. Most of their stuff was new; all of it was discounted.

I push-mowed the church lawn for a dollar a week. If my memory serves me right, the lawn was twenty or thirty acres. (This was back before the establishment of child labor laws and family protective agencies.) I used my hard-earned money to add to my matchbox car collection. They had a big selection down at the Bonanza store. Usually I would have enough money left over to buy a couple bottles of Orange Crush soda from the cooler at Jew Knight's Sinclair station. It was an old-fashioned store with a wooden floor, a wood-frame screen door, and the green dinosaur sign. Sometimes I would spend a summer morning collecting empties from ditches around the township and get a popsicle from Helen's Market.

One night, on the way back from town, we had an experience that has forever lodged itself in my mind. My sister and I were sitting in the back seat listening to my parents talk. Mom was in a good mood.

"I was able to get enough to have a nice meal each day," she said. "And we're only short meat for one meal."

Dad said, "Well, we'll just pray the Lord will provide that meat."

It seems to me that the words had barely escaped his mouth when a rabbit darted onto the road ahead of us. Dad let out an exclamation and there was a slight bump, and he braked the car to a stop. It was a spring night and the car lights shone down into the ditch. Dad backed up the car, jumped out, scrambled down into the ditch, bent down, and came up with a dazed rabbit. A sharp chop to the neck and he put his fresh kill into the trunk with the rest of the groceries.

Dad took the rabbit home and nailed it to a post in the basement and cleaned it, and we ate rabbit with potatoes and vegetables for dinner the next day. My sister and I avoided eating Peter Rabbit and filled up on the potatoes and vegetables.

My little brother Kevin was about three at the time. It must have made an impression on him. A few days later we were driving through town when a cat darted in front of the car. There was no way to miss him. Kevin was belted between my sister and me in the back seat.

"Oh, my, we ran over a cat," someone said. Kevin said, "Oh, no, that is gonna taste terrible."

Of course we didn't eat the cat... because the tires ruined all the good meat.

Growing up, things almost always seemed tight. We lived from week to week. But I don't ever remember going to bed hungry, and we rarely had to eat roadkill.

"I have been young, and now am old; yet I have not seen the righteous forsaken, nor his descendants begging bread" (Psalm 37:25).

Chapter 4
EMPTY PORCHES

My wife Lois grew up in Wolfe County, Kentucky, in the little village of Campton, where she was born. Campton likes to call itself "The Friendliest Little Town in the Mountains." It's more than a slogan. People really are friendly down there. It is situated in a beautiful part of the Bluegrass state. It's nicely out of the way. You have to mean to go there.

She lived the first nine years of her life in a white, two-bedroom house. It had a tin roof that rang in the rain and a porch, like any self-respecting Kentucky home. The house sat in the shadow of a mountain across the creek from the Campton Baptist Church. Last time I visited Campton the little house was still there. I think Lois still owns a twelfth of it.

Lois has fond memories of growing up in Campton—especially Sundays. The family attended the Baptist Church. After church they would always walk to their Mamaw Banks' place for chicken dinner and then down to the bus station for ice cream. Lois and her siblings would climb up on the stool at the soda fountain. Mamaw

Hatton would pay with some coins out of her little black change purse.

The rest of the afternoon and evening they would spend on their Mamaw Hatton's porch visiting with the neighbors and watching the traffic until evening came. The kids would get restless and play rowdy games in the yard. Mamaw Hatton would try valiantly to protect her beautiful petunias and impatiens from harm.

They never whiled away an evening on the porch without Ale-8 on hand. (In that part of the country, the soft drink of choice is a sweet ginger ale they call "Ale-8-One." The way Kentucky people say it, it sounds like "Al-Eight." My children always beg for it as soon as we get within sight of the mountains.)

Lois's mother is the kind who would not think of taking her children out in public without having them perfectly groomed. You can see this in all the pictures taken when Lois was a girl. Her dresses were spotless above her dimpled knees. Her hair was perfectly clean and cut with straight bangs above her dark eyes.

Their little house did not have hot running water, so to get four little children ready for church took some effort. Lois's mother bathed each of the children in turn in a washtub on the kitchen floor. She had to heat the bathwater on the stove. After their baths, they would brush their teeth and rinse their mouths with Listerine and spit in the tub. By the time they were all done, the water was, well, let's just say "used."

One Sunday morning she had the children all ready for church, bathed and dressed in their crisp Sunday-go-to-meetin' clothes. That was back in the day when little girls commonly wore white gloves and hats to church. They were just about to step out the door to walk to church, Bibles in hand, when disaster struck. Lois and her older brother Alvin begin to jostle one another. Little Lois lost her balance and tumbled into the washtub. Beyond her baptism that morning, there would be no more religious observances that day.

Lois has her own way of getting everybody up and ready and making the Lord's Day special.

Hats off to moms around the world today for all they do to point little eyes to God.

Lois's mother has a home in northern Indiana and her grandmothers have passed on. The porches are empty now.

Chapter 5
THE BEST PLACE TO DO THEOLOGY

I started to study theology at Moody Bible Institute in the fall of 1977. After a few distractions, I was awarded a master's degree in the spring of 2006. The fellowship, teaching, quiet enjoyment of the library, and the experience of the city are fond memories to me now.

Have you ever considered, though, that formal theological institutions are not the primary place God intends for people to learn? There is no institution on earth that is better equipped as a place of learning than the simplest Christian home. There are no professional teachers or professors who can have the impact that a father or a mother can have on a child in the home.

The idea that the primary place to learn theology is in high-arched halls of academia did not come from the Bible. Oh, any place is a good place to learn theology, including theological institutions, but the primary place God intends for us to learn theology is at our father's side, at our mother's feet, and in our Grandpa's lap.

Maybe the best context for learning God's truth is beside a generous piece of our grandmother's apple pie, hot from the oven, cooled by homemade vanilla ice cream and drizzled with caramel. According to Psalm 78 and Deuteronomy 6, home is the best place to learn theology. Home is where theology really sticks to your ribs. That is why we are commanded to do theology at home.

Last Thursday night we were lying in bed. Our six-year-old, Hope, joined us for a few minutes. Suddenly she popped up and said, "Hey, Dad, you know what I'm going to eat tomorrow?"

"No, Sweetie. What are you going to eat?"

"Fries," she said. "You wanna know why?"

"Why are you going to eat fries tomorrow?"

I asked. Then she flashed a smile, showing two missing teeth, and said with perfect timing and specific emphasis, "Because tomorrow is FRI-day."

She's learning lessons in humor and she hasn't ever been to a school.

The greatest Teacher that ever graced the earth changed the world by training a dozen men as they walked the lakeshore, camped out in the mountains, went fishing, and jostled through the city rubbing shoulders with raw humanity. That's the way it is at home. Learning just slips up on you when you aren't paying attention, and before you know it you have in your heart a lesson you will never forget. There are so many good things about home. One of them is that it is a great place to teach and learn the most important lessons in life. We try to learn together in our home every day.

Chapter 6
MY BAPTISM IN ORANGE POP

I spend a lot of time waiting for my family to get in the car so we can go places. One thing that keeps me from getting hostile about that is that I get to scare them by beeping the horn when they walk by the front of the van. It's just one of those little ways I save money on therapy.

We love to go places together. One summer evening we decided to go to town and grab a pizza for a little picnic. We picked up our pizza and some ice and pop and headed for the park. On the way we saw some radio-controlled model airplanes flying over a field. We drove over and parked to watch. It was a great spot for a family picnic.

We got out and set up our lawn chairs to watch the planes and enjoy our pizza. I got a big orange pop in one hand and a plate of about three thick slices of extra-cheese pizza in the other and settled into my lawn chair.

I was hungry. Every cell in my body was concentrating on devouring that pizza. My chair was sitting right in front of the grill of the van.

Our firstborn slipped into the van from the back door, stole quietly forward, and then—just as I put my big cup of orange pop up to my lips—he laid on the horns, which were about ten inches from my head.

I'm sure the little lawn chair was well over the legal load limit. When the horn sounded I lurched, and that baby instantly collapsed in a pile of twisted aluminum. I ended up on the ground. My family and a half-dozen strangers gathered around to belly laugh at me lying there with half an extra-cheese pizza on my chest and baptized in orange pop. I don't remember anyone helping me up. (They couldn't have done so without a block and tackle handy anyway.)

After the humiliation of that, as you can imagine, I had to leave town. I could never have been taken seriously as a man of the cloth in that town again.

You reap what you sow, and when you do reap and sow, the results will usually not be funny like my little story here.

Chapter 7
TROUBLE ON THE
KOKOSING GAP TRAIL

"You need to get more exercise," they said. But when you weigh as much as I did that's not as easy as it sounds. And on a perfectly innocent-looking day a few years ago, it landed me in trouble.

I had talked my then thirteen-year-old son Kyle into taking a bike ride with me. We were biking the Kokosing Gap Trail in Mt. Vernon, Ohio. It was a beautiful path along a river, built on an old railroad right-of-way. Most of the trail ran through a cool tunnel of shady trees. Kyle was riding his mountain bike. I had borrowed an antique brown, single-speed girl's bike from my wife. Bad idea.

We started at the trailhead in Mount Vernon and rode to Gambier. The village of Gambier is the home of an old Episcopal college that sits on a hill above the river. The shady streets are lined with old stone college buildings and tasteful homes. The college bookstore was a favorite spot for us. We stopped there for a cold drink before making our way back down to the trail.

The next village on the trail is Howard. We pedaled under a high stone arch where Route 36 passes high over the trail. The trail runs away from the river through corn and bean fields between Howard and Danville, where the trail ends. We planned to turn around there and make our way back. It would be fun to brag that we had biked the whole trail, but that was not to be.

About a mile from the end of the trail we ran into trouble. More accurately I ran into trouble. The bike I was riding was old and rusty and the chain broke. We were miles from the car. I needed some exercise but I didn't want that much. I didn't know what to do. It was a few miles to the nearest phone. No one was home at the time, even if we did get to the phone. If I called friends they would mock me forever for riding my wife's old bike and breaking the chain. I'd rather they find my body and conclude I died in some heroic struggle.

Suddenly an idea came to me. When you weigh over 250 pounds you have a big waist, and when you have a big waist you have a long belt.

My belt was long enough to use as a tow line. Kyle was willing. I handed him one end of the belt, I took the other, and he towed me all the way back to the car. It was really a nice ride.

I didn't even have to steer. I sat upright and took in the view. Kyle didn't let up all the way back to the car.

It was near dusk when we finally got back to the car. While we were putting the bikes back in the van, he said, "Hey, Dad. Why didn't you ride and pull me?" I smiled. Maybe I was fat, but I wasn't stupid.

When you are out there miles from home on the trail, it's nice to know you are not alone if you get into trouble. That's why it's a real good idea to travel in two's as often as you can.

I'm pretty sure Solomon never rode a bike, but he understood the value of a friend when you get in a fix. He said it like this: *"Two are better than one, because they have a good reward for their labor. For if they fall, one will lift up his companion. But woe to him who is alone when he falls, for he has no one to help him up"* (Ecclesiastes 4:9–10).

Chapter 8
TAKING A WALK

When a dad and a boy and a dog take a walk in the country, if the dad walks a mile, the boy walks two and the dog five. That was the way of things one autumn afternoon on the banks of the Kokosing. Kyle climbed on rocks. Our golden retriever Ginger chased her fancy up the hills and ran ahead scouting for us. Then she would circle back and trot panting at our side for a while before shooting off again. I walked with a stick, ambling slowly along enjoying the sound of water over rocks and the scent of autumn that hung in the air. The leaves were falling steadily into the water and along the bank. A couple hard frosts had brought on the color and loosened the leaves for fall.

A wall of rock ran up on our left. We walked northeast with the river on our right, following a fisherman's path. At one point Kyle left the dirt path and climbed up onto some rocks. They were covered with leaves and drying vegetation.

I was a few paces ahead when I heard him cry out. It was not a little call for help but a terrified scream. He had fallen into a hole obscured by brush. I looked back and I could see him clinging to the rock and trying to keep from falling farther into the hole. Later he told me that one of the reasons he was so frightened was that just before the ground gave way beneath his feet, he saw a snake slide into the hole.

When I looked back I could see that he had fallen down between two rocks into a hole about five feet deep. He had no way of knowing that his feet dangled only eight or ten inches from the ground. The frightened snake was no threat, and he was in no real danger. All this was immediately evident to me, but his cry was so desperate, so pitiful. I ran to him, bounded up on the rock and pulled him from the hole. The fear on his face and the desperation in his voice stirred my soul, even though I could see he was in no real danger. I was only rescuing him from his own panic. He clung to me for a moment with a hammering in his little chest.

We both enjoyed a good laugh when I showed him that he was never really in any danger.

We walked home. He walked a little closer to me on the way back. The sun was well on its way down the sky, and we decided it would be a good time to see what Mom was planning for supper.

I don't know about you, but I've had the bottom fall out on me a couple of times. It throws a scare into you. But the Word promises that the Lord will spring to the aid of his children when they cry out to him in desperation. He knows exactly how much danger we are in. He knows the fear that torments our hearts, and he knows the end from the beginning. So when the bottom falls out and we are plunged into fear, the right thing to do is cry out to our Father. Sometimes he will deliver us from danger. Sometimes he will deliver us from our own panic, and then we walk a little closer to him on the way home.

"I sought the LORD, and He heard me, and delivered me from all my fears" (Psalm 34:4).

Chapter 9
YODER, THE AMISH BEAGLE

Beagles are great dogs. They are bred to chase rabbits. But if there aren't any rabbits around, they will chase cats, cars, and boys. And if they are really bored, beagles have even been known to chase girls. Now the nice thing about beagles is that they are short and they stay short all their lives so they are just the right size for little boys. They are brown and black and white and they have long ears that flop when they run.

We wanted one. One day, driving the back roads in the Amish country of Ohio, we found one. We bought him from a nice Amish farmer, so we thought he should have a good Amish name. "Swartzentrooper" seemed a little cumbersome, and "Miller" was too plain, so we settled on "Yoder" in honor of some good Amish friends.

Yoder loved to romp with the kids. We took him with us on our full-moon walks and we even took him fishing once. We had a day of it.

He ran and romped and tumbled and hiked and played all day, and then on the way home he fell asleep in the car on Kyle's lap, spent from his exploits.

The sad fact is, days like that were rare for Yoder. Soon after the little dog came into our family, we moved to town and Yoder had to live on a chain in the backyard. We didn't like the arrangement. It was a beautiful house in a very nice part of town and the neighbors were delightful people, but we all longed for the country.

We were grateful for our home, but we began to pray regularly for a place in the country. We recorded the request in a prayer journal. In a few weeks our prayer was answered in a wonderful way. We were able to lease a nice old two-story farmhouse on a dead-end road. The house rested in an isolated valley.

Traffic was sparse. Unless someone was lost or coming for a visit, we had only two cars a day on our road. We had a daily visit from the mailman, which was an event. And every day or two a man from the gas company would check the well.

We let Yoder off his chain and let him run. He climbed hills, chased rabbits, swam in the creek and shadowed the kids on their explorations. He was in beagle heaven. If you had any imagination at all you could see the joy on his face. But his happy days would be few.

One rainy Saturday morning I was working at the study in town and I got a sad call from home. I came home right away. When I got out to the house the entire family was still in tears. Between sobs they told me what had happened.

The man had come as usual to check the gas well. As he was leaving, he looked over toward where the children were playing. I assume he was checking to see where they were, and when he was satisfied all was clear, he gunned the engine of his truck toward his next stop and drove away fast. But Yoder was still in the lane. The little dog was not visible over the hood of his truck.

He ran right over the dog in full view of the children. Kyle, who was about eleven at the time, ran to the lane, fell to his knees, and gathered his little dog to his chest. Yoder looked up at Kyle, let out a weak yelp, and died in his arms. Kyle carried Yoder over and laid him down in the straw of the corncrib where he usually slept.

When I got home I wrapped Yoder in a blanket and gathered him up and walked back to the creek to bury him there. All the children followed in a sad little procession of mourners. The mint grows there and it smells sweet in the spring. Yoder used to love to roll in it.

We all held hands and we each prayed and thanked God for bringing Yoder into our lives. Before we left, we made up our minds that from now on no matter what other people called the creek, we were going to call it Yoder Creek. Then we walked back home.

We all sat in the house and hurt and remembered our little pet. His life was so short. It still hurts a little to think that Yoder lived most of his life confined to a little circle defined by the length of his chain, and he really had only a few weeks of freedom his whole life.

This sad world is full of people running in circles. Their ability to experience the joys of life is limited by the chains of their own sin.

I remember a man like that. He had four beautiful children and a loyal wife who would have opened her heart to him. But he never tossed a ball with his son. He never walked on the beach with one of his beautiful daughters on his arm. He never held his grandchildren in his arms or watched them play ball or took them fishing because he was confined by the chains of drunkenness and pride. On the day of his funeral I looked at his body and thought he seemed weary from straining toward life on the end of a chain but never really living.

I guess I've been that way myself more than I like to admit—limited to a small circle defined by the length of my chain. That's the way our adversary the Devil wants it. He delights in seeing us continually defeated by sin and burdened with guilt. Jesus said Satan is a thief who came to steal, kill, and destroy. Satan wants to limit us by the chains of our unforgiveness, lust, greed, gluttony, impure speech, or other sins, and he is looking forward to our company in hell when we die.

But Jesus came to set the captives free. I don't know about you, but I intend to enjoy my freedom. Jesus paid for it with his life and I like to imagine he smiles when he sees me running free.

Chapter 10
LOUDENVILLE STREET FAIR

Autumn breaks the stranglehold of summer's heat. The corn dries and the fields slowly turn from green to golden. Birds flock and fly south. The air becomes clear and the sky bluer. The last flowers of the season bloom and farm markets spill over with bounty. Grains await the harvest, forming a patchwork quilt of field, pasture, and woods. These are days to be outdoors until the last streak of sunlight slips beyond the horizon.

One year when fall came to the hill country of Ohio, we set off in the family car to spend the day together. Our intent was just to follow the hood ornament. We might take in a farm market or antique store. We might visit a few craft shops or browse a book shop.

We drove north from Mount Vernon, Ohio, along State Route 3 through Amity and Jellico and along the Mohican River valley. Route 3 is a good road with wide, clear, elevated views of forest and farm. The colors were near their peak. Our intent was to follow Route 3 north to Loudenville and then travel east into Holmes County for the day. Maybe we would have Trail Bologna sandwiches and a dessert of coffee and cheese tarts. We never reached Holmes County.

Coming into Loudenville we were distracted by a banner stretched overhead that invited us to their annual street fair. Sights, sounds, and smells delighted the senses as we parked and strolled the streets of the quaint village. The Methodist women grilled onions, peppers, and sausage. The Jaycees supplied perfect buttery sweet corn. The pumpkin pie was the pride of the Presbyterians. One vendor sold roasted cinnamon almonds. The rides were simple. There were ponies for small children. A Ferris wheel lifted people high over the town. Delighted children rode the carousel waving chubby hands each time they passed their parents. Couples walked arm in arm. I sipped coffee and savored the day.

Down a side street we strolled among craft booths and shops. On the west end of the street, sweet music drifted up from an elderly man playing the fiddle. A choir made up of senior citizens was singing and we stopped to listen. They finished their number just as we arrived and slowly made their way off stage, leaving a single elderly man standing alone. He leaned on the corner of the piano. He wore a tweed cap and jacket and a hand-tied bow tie and his eyes shone while the introduction played. I'd never heard the song before or since but I have never forgotten it. It was an old ballad titled "O, I Wish I Was Eighteen Again." As the old gentleman sang, a stillness quieted the streets. The fair patrons stopped and listened until the song was done.

It seemed that no one moved until the last few notes of the song drifted out over the crowd like mist on the cool autumn air.

The old man smiled and tipped his cap to the applause. The people began to move again and chatter, and the children pulled their mothers toward rides, candy apples, and cotton candy.

We drove back along Route 3 over the Mohican and between fields of half-harvested corn, the way of migrating fowl. The moon rose with the early onset of dusk. We drove in silence. The old man's musical reminiscence stayed in my heart and moved me again to cherish life and savor all of its legitimate delights. The older I get the more often my thoughts are hushed like the crowd that day and I wish I was eighteen again.

David must have had similar thoughts. In the thirty-ninth Psalm he wrote: *". . . While I was musing, the fire burned. Then I spoke with my tongue: 'LORD, make me to know my end, and what is the measure of my days, that I may know how frail I am. Indeed, You have made my days as handbreadths, and my age is as nothing before You; certainly every man at his best state is but vapor. Selah. Surely every man walks about like a shadow; surely they busy themselves in vain; he heaps up riches, and does not know who will gather them. And now, Lord, what do I wait for? My hope is in You'* " *(Psalm 39:3–7).*

We have no hope of returning to live our youth again, but in Christ we do have a better hope, which is eternal. It is *". . . [the] hope of eternal life which God, who cannot lie, promised before time began" (Titus 1:2).*

Chapter 11
FULL-MOON WALKS

In our local library is a delightful children's book called Owl Moon. It's about a little girl and her daddy walking through the snow on a winter night to see an owl. Somewhere, in some city, a grown-up girl thinks about her daddy bundling up a little girl years ago and making a memory while field on field of fresh snow reflected the moon's luminous glow. She writes her memory down and adds full-color illustrations and thousands of us enjoy the walk with her. A wise man. A blessed little girl.

We have a tradition in our home. We call it the "moon walk," but it's not what you might think. It is not a dance step. (We're card-carrying Baptists and don't go in for any kind of dancing. When I was a boy I would even get a note to excuse me from square dancing in gym class. The first Baptist preacher, John the Baptist, lost his head at a dance so, you see, we Baptists have a healthy aversion to them.) The deal is, I promised the kids that on full-moon nights they don't have to go to bed until I take them on a walk by the light of the moon. They love this tradition. I love it more.

It started years ago on a cool fall night when Yoder, our beagle, now gone to his doggie reward, was just a tiny pup. It was a Saturday night and I picked up my walking stick to go out into the night and pray and prepare my heart for the Lord's Day. Kyle asked to go along. Yoder insisted on coming too. The moon was big and bright and the air cool. We walked past tall corn ripening for harvest along a wide grassy waterway. We talked to the Lord as we walked. We followed a lane cut through a wood like a dark tunnel shaded from the moonlight. It opened into an arch of misty light at the other end.

I made the comment on the way back to the house, "We ought to take a walk every time there is a full moon." That's how it became a tradition for years.

One night we sauntered back the long limestone lane across the road to discover our delightful neighbors. They insisted on showing us around their tidy farm and then "forced" us to gather around their big oak table and enjoy ice cream and strawberries. They insisted that we enjoy generous seconds and you can't be too careful about relations with your neighbors.

We found them to be good, country people. A couple hours later we said our good-byes and sauntered back home in the cool midsummer night.

When dozens of things that we spent hundreds of dollars on are long forgotten, we will all still remember our moon walks. King's Island and Cedar Point don't have anything like that. From a moon walk a few years ago I have a snapshot in the album of my memory of a path of light cast by the moon on a surface of a mountain lake.

One night Hope and I strolled under a full September moon along the shore of the straits of Mackinac. I walked with her little hand in mine while we listened to the rhythmic lapping of the water on the beach and the faint ringing of a bell out in the harbor.

I think the reason we love our walks so much is simply because we love being together. I love to be with the children talking quietly or just walking along in sweet quietness until the sounds of the night calm our spirits. Usually we just tramp along pulling cool night air into our lungs. On our moon walks words aren't always needed.

- The music of a spring leaping from a hillside in the springtime
- Cricket and frog duets in the summer
- Leaves crumpling underfoot in the fall
- The dappled pattern on the road ahead of us that moonlight makes shining through the trees
- The crunch of frozen ground in winter
- The wind blowing across an open field
- Stirring in the leaves of a big oak beside the road
- A plane droning its way across the vast night sky
- The lonely sound of a truck grinding its way across the valley
- Walking sticks tapping on the road

- Blinking fireflies
- The perfume of new-mown hay

But these little delights are extras. The real joy of a moon walk is being with those we love—listening to each other and listening with each other. I love to be with them and I love it that they love to be with me. And sometimes on our night walks I peer into the endless night sky past a thousand stars and out into the place where God dwells alone and I am awed that he loves to be with me and that he loves it that I love to be with him!

"You are worthy, O Lord, to receive glory and honor and power; for You created all things, and by Your will they exist and were created" (Revelation 4:11).

"O LORD, our Lord, how excellent is Your name in all the earth, who have set Your glory above the heavens! . . . When I consider Your heavens, the work of Your fingers, the moon and the stars, which You have ordained, what is man that You are mindful of him, and the son of man that You visit him? . . . O LORD, our Lord, how excellent is Your name in all the earth!" (Psalm 8:1, 3–4, 9).

Chapter 12
THE FIREFLY EFFECT

My sweetest childhood memories are of simple things like the tire swing in the big oak out front, playing catch with my dad, and swimming in the creek. Another of those simple things was chasing fireflies on the lawn as night fell on a summer evening. The bugs had only a small light, but they were especially brilliant because of the dark backdrop of the night sky.

Some lights guide us to safety, like lights on a runway or lighthouses. Lights can stir up feelings of warm security, like the soft light falling out of your window at home reminding you that someone you love is waiting for you. Lights can even have healing power, like the beam of light used in laser surgery. When a ray of light is focused it can warm and heal or start a destructive fire. There is an indescribable value to the light of a wood fire, whether outdoors or burning on your own hearth. Who doesn't love peering into the light of a campfire on a cool evening outdoors?

The culture in which we are raising our families is morally and spiritually very dark. We live in a time when the new lows of human depravity are being graphically displayed in media. This is true all over the world and in almost every community on earth. Not even isolated rural communities are exempt.

The ways of God are ignored and the laws of God are violated by millions. Morally and spiritually, we live in a dark hour. We wrestle against the "rulers of the darkness of this age." Spiritual light is as rare as it is beautiful. Jesus told his followers to let their light so shine that men will see their good works and glorify their Father in heaven. Paul said that those who do all things without complaining are blameless and harmless, children of God without fault in the midst of a crooked and perverse generation, among whom we shine as lights in the world, holding fast the word of life.

There is a principle, though, that warms the heart and gives hope to those who feel overwhelmed by the dark hour in which we live. One way to state the principle is like this:"The darker the night the brighter the light shines."

Even the smallest light is noticeable if it is dark enough outside. That is what I like to call the "Firefly Effect." It makes me hopeful.

The spring of my seventeenth year I heard that there was a preacher at Immanuel Baptist Church in Arcanum, Ohio. I got my dad's powder blue VW Superbeetle and drove to the service. I was hungry for truth and I wasn't turned away empty. I don't remember the name of the guest preacher. I do remember a number of the things he said.

One thing he said was, "The flower of youth never appears more beautiful than when it bends toward the Sun of Righteousness."

I have remembered that all my life. I wish I remembered the name of the preacher who said it. I just did a quick search on the wonderful Internet and discovered that the quote was originally the work of Matthew Henry, an English divine who lived from 1662 to 1714. So people have noticed outstanding young people throughout time.

I was interested to discover that I had remembered it exactly word for word, even though that was nearly thirty years ago. I still remember it and it is a timeless truth. I have rarely spoken to a group of young people without reminding them of the truth.

When I was at Moody Bible Institute studying in the graduate school, I heard a story that touched my heart. Mayor Daley once made this comment to Joe Stowell, the president of Moody: "In August, when the Moody students return to Chicago, it's like the lights come on all over the city." That night, back in my room alone, I looked out over the great city all alight and considered the beauty of the analogy.

Once, in conversation with Flint's Mayor James Rutherford, he made a similar comment to me about the ministry of the Character Inn. He said, "We see your organization like the crown jewel of the downtown." Imagine that, the Firefly Effect at work in Chicago and even in downtown Flint, Michigan. Wherever on earth even the smallest light of faith exists, the deepest darkness cannot overcome it. Darkness only serves to amplify the beauty of the light.

"But you are a chosen generation, a royal priesthood, a holy nation, His own special people, that you may proclaim the praises of Him who called you out of darkness into His marvelous light" (I Peter 2:9).

Chapter 13
HEIDI'S SWING

Today I took Hope for a walk in the arboretum near our house. We watched the water run over rocks beneath one of the little stone footbridges. We saw butterflies and listened to new birdsongs. We saw trees in the bud and in the blossom. (The dogwoods opened this weekend. That calls for celebration.) I held Hope's soft chubby hand and we looked at tiny violets and dandelions. Hope thinks dandelions are beautiful flowers and gathered a bouquet for Mom. She doesn't know that most people consider them a nuisance.

She is just now three. I remember when Heidi was her size. Now Heidi is a tall, graceful young woman.

When Heidi was three or four we had the world's greatest tree swing. The swing was high in the branches of a Chinese elm that grew at the corner of our big country house in Knox County. The swing must have been at least fifteen feet up in the tree.

The children have never collected toys like some kids do. They play with one another and cook up fun things to do. They would play in the creek and tumble in the field and explore the barn, but Heidi's favorite plaything was the swing.

We all enjoyed the swing, but Heidi especially loved it. She would ride the swing for hours and cry if you took her off. She would cry "Higher, higher!" I have in my memory a picture of her in a jumper, her blonde hair blowing in the wind, eyes as blue as the sky, pumping her little bare legs. You couldn't push the swing high enough to satisfy her. I would push her until the rope slacked and her toes touched the branches of the tree (but only if her mother was not looking).

One day I was mowing with a brush hog behind a big Farmall H and hooked the swing with the fender of the tractor. I couldn't stop in time and I pulled the swing down, along with the entire branch it was tied to. It came down so easily that I have always wondered if it was rotten and ready to come down at any time anyway. When we hung the swing back up we had to use a branch much closer to the ground so it was about a third of its original size.

They don't make a video game that touches that swing. Cedar Point will never build a ride to rival it.

Someday maybe Heidi will have a child of her own. I hope the Lord blesses her with a dozen. She will take them out back and swing them in a swing or take them for a walk in the park. I hope her mind goes back over the years and across the miles to the backyard of the old farmhouse on Rutledge Road. Only then will she realize the joy she brought to my heart.

Chapter 14
BETWEEN MEMORIAL DAY
AND LABOR DAY

Memorial Day and Labor Day are the bookends of summer. This morning I found a couple old journal entries I had written the summer our oldest was only about six. The first one was written at the end of the day on Memorial Day; the second was written after I put the children to bed on Labor Day.

"Memorial Day is nearly over. The speeches and parades and remembrances at the cemetery are past and so are the backyard grill-out and the family ball game. As a child I never would have thought to feel quietly sentimental on an evening like this, but as I sip a cup of herb tea this evening I have a sense of anticipation. Memorial Day is a kind of passage into summer. This week will be the last of school, and lengthening days will move the family out into the garden and the flower beds and the porch.

"We will enjoy the sunsets and birdsongs and smell the flowers and freshly cut grass. We will listen to the enchanting sounds of summer nightfall. We will stay up later and feel closer as a family. There will be more time to laugh and play together, to teach Holly to hit a baseball and throw—not "like a girl." We will take some trips, hopefully, with a little variety. We will notice natural beauty and linger at points of historical import and spend less time this year at the "traps" that leave you feeling empty and defrauded.

"The children love nothing more than an unhurried time of swinging and sliding and merry-go-rounding at the park. We're going to ride bikes and foot race and hold hands and walk barefoot along the beach and look into each other's eyes more this summer.

"In short we are going to do the things we will be glad we did twenty years from now. We are going to grow our tomatoes and eat them like apples on summer afternoons. We are going to grow a patch of sweet, sweet, sweet corn and gobble it with butter dripping off of our chins, and we're not going to worry about cholesterol.

"It is so hard not to spend our lives getting ready to live, always getting ready to go and never really going."

That summer and the twenty summers that have followed it passed swiftly like the one we just enjoyed. At the end of the summer I found another journal entry:"I just returned from the children's rooms and my heart is full. The summer is now officially over. Memorial Day is gone and Labor Day has come and gone and the days in between flew by in a whir. We were not able to do all the things we wanted to do this summer but it has been a full one.

"Today I took my precious little Holly's training wheels off her bike and we all laughed as we watched her wobble through the yard and around the driveway. She still throws like a girl and always will.

"Last night Kyle ran into a telephone pole and almost knocked his two upper front teeth out. His nose swelled up and this morning while flying through the yard on his bike he nearly finished the job of removing his teeth. (I was secretly relieved that they didn't come out yet because I don't have a penny to slip under his pillow.) Chuck was sitting up in his bed with a pillow propped up behind his head reading a book, 'cause that's what Dad does.

Heidi pronounces cookies with a *th* sound on the end.

"After a day of running and jumping and riding and tussling and picnicking at Grandma and Grandpa's, they all tumbled willingly into bed and by now I'm sure they are all in their own little dream worlds. I just hope tonight their little hearts and dreams are as full and happy as mine. I'm sure there isn't a dad in the world that is any more grateful to God for his little ones than I am.

"The last day of summer slipped away today and each day is becoming more fall-like. Tonight we have traveled another passage of life and we all crawl into bed with our hearts full of happiness and our minds full of plans for tomorrow."

Chapter 15
VANISHING ARTS

I'm not one for conspiracy theories. I hate blaming everything from the breakdown of the American home to global warming on the liberal media and television. But I must say I really do believe the television and other factors are contributing to the vanishing of what I like to call the quaint and mostly rural arts.

Skipping, whittling, whistling, yodeling, playing the harmonica, storytelling, baking homemade bread, quilting, juggling, and singing harmony are what I consider vanishing arts. These are the kinds of things you do together at home out on the porch on a summer's eve. They are the kinds of things you do around the fire in the winter. These are the kinds of things you do together in the most sacred of all the rooms of the house, the kitchen (with the exception of skipping, which my wife and my mother agree had better be done outdoors).

The vanishing arts usually require conversation or interaction or the kind of quiet that binds your soul together with others. The vanishing arts have to be treasured and protected and passed down through the generations like a grandfather clock from the Old Country. I believe when one of the vanishing arts is bequeathed from one generation to the next something good happens. Along with the skill or knowledge, other things of value are transferred. Appreciation, affirmation, and affection we all crave are communicated in a sacred, often wordless way. Our hands touch; our eyes meet; our souls are nurtured in the exchange.

Prayer is a vanishing art in many homes. Consider this: What do you think is better for the soul of a young boy—a half-hour watching a funny television program where the lead character is a practicing homosexual—or a season of prayer on his knees with his mom and dad and brothers and sisters?

There are forces and factors at work that are contributing to the loss of these beautiful and soul-enriching arts. The pace of modern life works against them. It is so much faster to snatch a box of frozen treats shaped like action heroes from the store than it is to get out a homemade ice cream maker. It is so much more convenient to stop at the gas station and grab a loaf of brown-colored bread, two for a dollar, than it is to grind wheat and make bread dough and wait for it to rise and bake it at home.

Even with all the conveniences of modern life we find it necessary to do so much away from home and away from each other. So much of what our children learn we depend on someone else to teach them away from home. This necessarily separates our families. We each have our own agenda for the day and often our agendas don't include each other. If we don't have time to spend more than a few minutes a day in intimate conversation with our children, it is unlikely that we are going to be able to find time for Grandma to teach us her favorite quilt pattern. If we have something scheduled every night of the week we will fancy ourselves too busy to listen to Grandpa sing the seventh verse of "The Old Rock Candy Mountain."

I read an interesting book about a fella who protested the pace of modern life by hiking all the way to the state capitol to turn in his driver's license. It was his symbolic, quiet protest to a pressure I fully understand. I found it humorously ironic, though, that he wrote about his walk and the book was printed and distributed using the most modern of means. I'm sure his royalty check was generated with the help of a computer, and the printing press itself was an advance in technology so profound that it fueled the Reformation and changed the world forever. So don't think of me as a Luddite or Neo-Amish.

I am writing this little nostalgic piece on a state-of-the-art computer, and I just enjoyed taking care of my morning necessaries a few steps from where I slept in perfect warmth and comfort. I enjoyed the luxury of a hot shower, and in a few minutes I will go down to the kitchen and have a bowl of hot oatmeal and steaming hot, fresh gourmet coffee, so I do have an appreciation for modern things.

I'm glad I didn't have to use an outdoor privy, write on a legal pad, and bathe in a washtub, heating my water on a woodstove. But still I like to look across the room in the evening and see my boys concentrating on a new chess opening instead of playing a video game.

I don't like the idea of my daughters spending the evening filling their minds with the latest politically correct propaganda masquerading as a situation comedy. Breaking down a young person's God-given inhibitions about things sacred to marriage is not something I consider to be entertaining or particularly funny. I would much rather look across the room on a winter evening and see them stitching on a beautiful quilt that will still be in the family after I am just a memory to them. I would rather hear them singing in the kitchen together while they are making "snickerdoodles" or oatmeal cookies.

I don't mind the kids using the computer, but I'm glad they wouldn't think of using it to chat online with someone whose hidden agenda is to defraud and defile. It pleases me to see my daughter using the PC to compose a newsletter about home, faith, and family and share a new granola recipe or instructions about a craft project that she did with her sisters.

Understand, I'm not ready to throw my computer in the dumpster. I don't want to stumble around the house in the dark at night or have to do my early morning writing by the light of a kerosene lamp. I don't want Lois to have to scrub my clothes clean on a washboard. I'm sort of attached to my permanent press shirts, and I would miss our DVD of *Anne of Green Gables*. I would be lost without e-mail. I don't want to go back in time, but I do plan to use the modern technology I enjoy to help my children grow to appreciate the quaint and mostly rural arts.

I want them to grow up with warm memories of home, skipping, playing the guitar, whistling, quilting, reading, and who knows, maybe even yodeling. I want them to have memories of quiet evenings together cultivating graceful arts and useful skills. I want them to know the simple pleasure of a game of checkers with Dad on a winter night.

Chapter 16
THE LOST ART OF SKIPPING

In a bookstore one evening I saw a round-headed, clear-eyed little black boy about seven years old skipping easily through the aisles. He was an adorable little fella and he appeared happy and carefree. He reminded me of a curly-haired little guy in our church named Andrew.

One summer I was speaking at a camp near Traverse City, Michigan, and Andrew was a camper that week. One afternoon I noticed him making his way across the campgrounds. Enjoying the shade of a large maple, I watched him from a distance. He must have had a treat from the Snack Shack in mind, because he had a big smile on his face and he was skipping all the way across the campground. He looked happy and carefree. He didn't seem to have a bit of self-consciousness about him. He was a pretty good little skipper too.

Something in me envies a carefree little boy with his dog on a summer afternoon. John Greenleaf Whittier noticed a little boy one summer afternoon and crafted his musings into poetic form:

"Blessings on thee, little man,

Barefoot boy, with cheek of tan!
With thy turned-up pantaloons,
And thy merry whistled tunes;
With thy red lip, redder still
Kissed by strawberries on the hill;
With the sunshine on thy face,
Through thy torn brim's jaunty grace;
From my heart I give thee joy,
I was once a barefoot boy!"

It's sad to think that most little boys probably stop skipping by the time they are twelve or thirteen. Soon thereafter they are slowed by the burdens of manhood. It's good they don't understand about taxes, unions, retirement plans, tuition, car payments, insurance premiums, and co-payments.

If we were able to help them understand how short and few their carefree summer days would be, they would probably stop skipping sooner.

Andrew probably has only about four more skipping summers left. Maybe if we changed the name of skipping to "hop-jogging" or something, little boys would keep doing it into adulthood. I have a little advice for you, Andrew. Skip on while you can, little man.

One balmy summer evening I was having a quiet talk with my dad on the porch of our country home. He got a faraway look in his eyes and made a statement that made me realize he had similar thoughts. He said, "The days you can throw everything you own in the trunk of the car and head off across the country will be gone before you know it. You should enjoy them a little while you can." He was right.

Some day soon I'm going to find an isolated stretch of beach, take off my shoes, and skip for a mile right along the place where the water laps the sand. I just hope nobody sees me.

Chapter 17
RED DOT DAYS

The house is quiet. Soft instrumental music floats easily from the speakers in the dining room. Candles burn on the mantel and on the table. The home is filled with a pleasing aroma. The children are reading, except for the second-oldest boy, who is concentrating on a game of chess with Dad. Mom is working with the girls on a beautiful quilt. It will be a gift for a favorite missionary couple in Alaska. Dinner has been cleared away and the oldest girl is now setting the table for a very special dessert. It is a cake with pineapple and orange frosting. Coffee for Dad and the older boys tonight is a special almond flavor; the scent of it wanders around the house.

The phone rings, but the ringer is low and no one moves to answer it. Before bedtime the music will quiet and the games and dishes will be cleared away. The family will gather in front of the fire and enjoy a time of prayer and sharing.

Hearts will be opened and Dad will read from the Bible. Then everyone will kneel for prayer before bedtime for the younger ones.

The older ones will spend another hour reading a classic novel aloud. Mom works on some thank-you cards. When the fire burns low the family secures the house for the night.

It has not always been this way. A few months ago this same family rarely ate a meal together. Everyone had their organizations and events, church, hobbies, community, and school; there was no time to be a family.

One fall day in a campground in Kentucky the family sat around a fire and discussed the direction they had been taking. Earlier that day they had been looking at memory books and photos of the family. It was a bittersweet time. The pictures were a painful documentation of how the sweet days of childhood slip away.

Their times to be together as a whole family were quickly slipping away. If any changes were going to be made, they would have to be made soon. That night as Mom and Dad lay in their sleeping bag, they prayed. They prayed that somehow God would allow them to have more times like their autumn weekend in the mountains. They prayed that they would have more times all together as a family, with no distractions, or interruptions, plenty of talk, just being together, laughter and time to pray and talk about important things. They prayed for more time to cement into place in the hearts of the children the things that were important.

Soon the tent was quiet except for the children's soft breathing. Outside the tent a softer whisper of wind in the pines on the ridge overhead, crickets, frogs, and the constant gurgle of the water winding over rocks in the stream lulled most of the family into sleep.

Dad got up quietly and slipped on a sweatshirt. He walked along the stream until he found a stump where he had started the day with his Bible. His soul was very quiet and he had a clear sense that something vital was going on inside his heart. He leaned back his head and drank in the dark outline of the mountain against the night sky.

Since he had been a little boy lying on the front porch of his grandfather's farmhouse he had always thought about the vastness of God when he gazed into the night sky. It was a cloudless night and the stars were brilliant overhead. He breathed slowly and let his lungs fill over and over again with the cool, fresh mountain air. He felt as if every breath expelled more of the frustration and confusion that had clouded his heart over the past months.

He was busy and felt that he was not in control of his life. He tried to deny it, but when he was honest, he knew that his family was slowly growing apart. They were all going their separate ways, pursuing their own interests. They were passing like ships in the night on their way to distant places.

Late that night in the mountains, a vision formed in his soul.

As he gazed into the starry heavens everything became clear. He knew what he would do. He stayed out listening to the music of nature, the owls, the brook, and the night insects for another hour. He spoke quietly with God, making vows as serious and as binding as he had ever made, and he knew from that night forward things would never be quite the same again.

Before he made his way slowly back down the mountain he knelt and prayed aloud.

"Oh, God," he begged, "forgive me for my foolish pursuit of empty things. Forgive me for my selfishness. Forgive me for ever thinking that I could compensate for the emptiness in my soul by filling my garage with toys. Forgive me for ever thinking that the gifts and privileges I buy for my children can ever replace my time and my love for them. Forgive me for worshiping things and using people and neglecting you. I repent."

Tears ran down his upturned face.

"Let my children see how much I love you. Let them see how much I love their mother. Let them see how I love each of them more than life itself."

When he rose from his knees his heart was light and his mind was clear. He made up his mind that he would not talk about what he had purposed in his heart to do that night, but when he got back to town, changes were made. He began to say no more. He chose to do without a number of the expensive trinkets that forced him to work overtime. He resigned from a board and a couple of organizations. He sold some things and took a load of unused things to the Goodwill. He organized his life and his schedule and made time for the most important things in his life and the most important people. The changes caught on. With a little encouragement the children began to throttle back on their outside pursuits.

A week after they returned home he stopped at the office supply store on the way home from work and bought a little package of adhesive red dots.

Those red dots would change his life. That night they all sat in the living room and marked a day a week on the calendar with the red dots. No one would accept any appointments or outside engagements on Red Dot Days. The phone would not be answered on Red Dot Days. The television would stay off on Red Dot Days. No one would go out and no one would be invited over. Red Dot Days were sacred family times set aside for the family alone. The girls would always plan special food and the boys made sure there was wood for the fire. Mom always tried to create a special atmosphere in the home for family nights. In the summer they made a deal with themselves that they would watch the sun set on Lake Michigan at least ten times.

Over the years the family collected a whole cupboard of games and a heart full of treasured memories.

All of the children will grow up and leave home and form families of their own. Each of the children will cherish memories of those simple, quiet, unhurried family times. Each of them will have Red Dot Days with their own families. And years from now when the driveway fills with cars and the grandchildren scamper in with their cheeks all aglow with the cold and excitement of a holiday, the Red Dot Days are what the family will remember most. Old photos and old videos will come out again, and the tears will flow. They will sing the old songs and laugh and cry and stay up late. They will remember the nights that bound them together in love, forged their character, and laid the foundation for their values.

And the house will quiet in the evening and all the grandchildren will circle their grandfather, and he will weave a tale that will keep them all silent in wonder. Before the fire dies on the hearth he will tell his favorite story about a quiet starry autumn night on a mountain in Kentucky many years ago. And then they will kneel together and pray.

Chapter 18
TOURIST ATTRACTION

We once lived in Ohio less than an hour from Holmes County, the largest Amish-Mennonite settlement in the world. Holmes County was often our day-off destination. Sometimes we would create a field trip to a farm or dairy or business. More often we would just leisurely drive the back roads. We took pictures of the children, picked apples, scouted for bittersweet, or shopped for Sweet Anne, which filled the car with fragrance. We frequented every craft store known to man and not a few bookstores.

At lunchtime we would buy what we needed for a picnic. Good cheese was abundant and cheap. It was a treat on homemade bread. On special occasions we would enjoy homestyle cooking at one of the wholesome eateries featuring roast beef, chicken, mashed potatoes and gravy, corn, dressing, fresh-baked bread with crocks of apple butter, and always a variety of homemade pies to choose from.

A couple times we rented a cabin overlooking a valley with a creek running along its bottom. In the evening we would sit around a fire, eat popcorn, chat with guests from other places around the Midwest, or just silently watch horse-drawn buggies clop-clop through the valley.

At night I slept in the loft with the children. Before sleep we lay in the darkness enjoying the warmth of the fire. I told them stories, prayed with them, and then played my harmonica to put them to sleep. What a sweet thing it would be to have them all small again in that loft all snug in their flannel gowns and PJs.

In the morning an Amish girl would bring coffee and huge pastries to the door of the cabin. We would stir the fire and enjoy a slow breakfast and morning Bible reading together.

We spent hours admiring impeccable white homes big enough for families our size and farms set among graceful hills. Once we stopped at a farm where an elderly Amish farmer made hickory rockers. Once we visited a farm market where shy children sold pumpkins, squash, and Indian corn. One of my favorite pictures is a picture of the children standing around a beautifully restored tractor on one of those carefree days.

We spent time admiring hand-sewn quilts and woodwork. We gazed on perfect gardens and groomed yards. We slowed to watch an Amish girl shave her lawn with a push mower.

A favorite stop was a bakery near the village of Charm in the Doughty Valley, where an Amish woman sold delicious lemon, raspberry, blackberry, and cherry cheese tarts. (What I wouldn't give for one of those with a cup of strong black coffee right now.)

Those trips to the Amish country reinforced a conviction that had been forming in our hearts for years. We longed for a close-knit family. We aspired to simplicity, to find joy and satisfaction in unadorned family life, to withstand the corrupting influence of worldly values and philosophies.

Our hearts were settling on a vision of a place where small vulnerable children are sheltered from the influences that would defile them or turn their hearts away from their family. We were committed to a home where the role of homemaker is respected and brothers and sisters are trained together in the ways of God every day.

It is easy to tell that we were not alone in our interest and admiration for the Amish way of life. Amish communities draw thousands of visitors every weekend.

Sitting on the porch one day I got to thinking about that. We live in an interesting time. In modern America simple family life is such a novelty that it has become a tourist attraction.

Chapter 19
REGULAR MAINTENANCE

The house is quiet. There are sounds that children make when they are sleeping; there is the gurgle and bumping of the water traveling through the heater pipes. I'm in the upstairs master bedroom. Lois will join me soon for a long winter's nap and set the fan to whirring. But right now things are quiet. An occasional car purrs through the neighborhood, only a few an hour this late in the evening.

We once lived in an old farmhouse at the end of a long lane in a valley surrounded by fields and woods and trees, birds and rabbits, deer, possums, groundhogs, skunks, and raccoons. We woke up every morning to the sound of the mourning dove in the high pines in the front yard and a hundred birdsongs. Our bedroom was on the first level. My study was on the second level in a garret. The children's rooms were also on the second level.

A screen porch wrapped around our bedroom, and on a midsummer night when it was cool enough, you could turn off the fan and open both doors to the screen porch and listen to the night sounds. I once read an essay about crickets that gave a formula for calculating the temperature by listening to how far apart the chirps were. Usually I just crawl out of bed and go over to the window and read the thermometer. I don't remember the equation, but I do know no one hermetically sealed into central air conditioning could have slept more peacefully.

There is one noise here that I don't remember hearing anywhere else. It is a steady, rhythmic ticking of a wall clock hanging over my dresser.

We've had it for nearly twenty years. It was a gift to Lois on our second Christmas together. It was a great improvement on the first gift I gave her, a pink wool suit that she tried hard to convince me she liked.

The clock has to be wound regularly. That is a problem for me. I like low-maintenance things. I had an ivy plant at college. I think I bought it at a garage sale the summer after my senior year in high school. Thought it would look good in my dorm room. Touch of home. I never had a plant before, but it seemed like a good idea— soft classical music, two serious scholars, and a thriving dorm plant.

My roommate was one of those types who always changes his oil every 2,000 miles, gets regular reviews of his insurance coverage, brushes between meals, and fastidiously types his class notes between lectures.

After walking past my struggling plant for a fortnight, he took pity on it and began to give it water. It drank like a thirsty man. Within a few days the plant took new life. A week later Paul (who always wears galoshes on rainy days) adopted the plant and put it over on his side of the room in the window.

Before the end of the term it had gone from peeking over the edge of the pot to climbing confidently up the window and was as bushy as the hair on the guys in your 1970s high school yearbook.

Regular maintenance is a cool thing. I gotta work on that. My dad once asked me if my car battery was a no-maintenance battery. I answered with a question:"Aren't all car batteries no-maintenance?"

I digress. Let me finish telling you about the clock. The clock stopped working dependably when it was a few years old. We kept it for sentimental value and, like they say, it still told the right time twice a day, but other than looking nice to people who drove by on the road outside, it had little value. So for years we faithfully dragged it wherever we moved and dutifully hung it on the wall.

On an excursion through Holmes County in Ohio one mellow fall afternoon, we followed a winding, hilly road into the tiny village of Farmerstown, where we happened on a little clock shop. The proprietor was an orderly, businesslike Amish man. He didn't make house calls, so we arranged an appointment for our ailing timepiece.

On a return trip, exploratory surgery revealed the damage—rust on the mainspring. Analogous to human heart disease, I suppose. And the prognosis: full recovery after surgery and a mainspring transplant. For the first time in years we parted briefly with the clock and drove quietly away. The man worked his work, and when we traced our way back the country lanes again we found our treasure waiting for us in good health. With regular winding and good maintenance, it's now more than a sentimental thing of beauty; it is a working clock and it provides a little company on a cold winter night when you are waiting for your wife to help you warm the bed.

In that sweet, warm, relaxing few minutes before you sink into untroubled winter sleep, it occurs to me that some of the most valuable things in life will never yield their best to us, and we will never know their best, without regular maintenance.

Since we live in a fallen world, the mainsprings of our lives, our marriages—our relationships—need a little review from time to time. Without regular checkups and quiet talks, without patient listening and regular consultations of the owner's manual, things are almost certain to wind down and disappoint.

Chapter 20
MOUNTAINTOP
AND MARKETPLACE

When I was a boy I hated having to go to bed. I still try to milk every minute of life out of every day, but I have grown to love the sweetness of sleep. On a good night I could sleep soundly through a tornado or a train wreck.

One night I was enjoying my usual sweet, sound sleep. It was a deep winter sleep under heavy quilts in a soft bed late at night after a taxing day. Suddenly I was awake. Lois was standing at the foot of the bed shouting, "Get up! Get up! Something's wrong." I don't know how long she shouted until I woke up.

"The whole house is shaking. Something's wrong!" she shouted. It was two or three o'clock in the morning and I was not awake enough to think clearly. "It's just a helicopter," I said. She was completely unsatisfied with my answer.

"No, Ken," she shouted, "it's not a helicopter, it's the furnace. Do something. I'm afraid. Do something before it blows up and kills us all."

When I finally staggered out of bed I realized the whole house was shaking. I walked into the living room and she was right. It was the furnace.

I said, "Lois, wait here," mostly because if she followed me to the basement she would realize I hadn't the foggiest notion of what to do to stop a shaking furnace. I went down the stairs and walked around it, scratching my head. On the side of the furnace was a switch that looked like a light switch. I turned it off. When I did, the shaking stopped. The switch was for the blower. The furnace was still firing and heat was radiating upward, so I went back to bed. I would call my Uncle Bill for free advice in the morning.

In the morning I returned to the basement with my furnace-repairman uncle on the other end of a cordless phone to offer tech support. I took a screwdriver and began to take apart the furnace. When I did, the source of the trouble immediately became obvious. The removal of the panel exposed the blower, which looked to me remarkably like a hamster wheel. Ironically, the wheel contained the carcass of a huge rat. He had crawled into the wheel, and when the blower had kicked on, obviously he could not keep up to speed. He paid for it with his life. What a way to go, I thought.

He was big enough to throw the blower out of balance and shake the whole house, including the bed where we were enjoying a long winter's nap. I delicately disposed of the big rat cadaver, put the panel back on the furnace, flipped the switch. The blower kicked in and ran smooth as butter.

It doesn't take much to throw things out of balance— just a little weight in the wrong place and things get ugly. Life is like that.

If I'm not careful, my family can get out of balance. We can retreat from the world in a way that displeases God and makes ministry impossible. Other times we can be so involved in helping other families that our family has little to give and nothing to say. We have to keep a careful balance between time on the mountaintop and time in the marketplace. Jesus did not spend all his time in ministry. He often went to a wilderness retreat or a garden. Some nights he stayed out alone under the stars all night on a mountain overlooking his beloved Jerusalem. Often he went to the wilderness with a few others. Sometimes Jesus retreated to the water to be alone for prayer and preparation.

Jesus did not spend all his time in isolation though. He loved to be among the people, and the sight of crowds usually moved him to tears. He spent hours moving among the people healing and helping, counseling and saving people who were laden with heartaches and sin. He displayed a perfect balance between the mountaintop and the marketplace, between the wilderness and the work.

Balance is important. Every family should have a family ministry in the marketplace and every family should have a rich and regular devotional experience. Every believer should spend some time on the mountaintop with the Lord and in the marketplace with people.

When I spend too much time in the wilderness or too much time in the marketplace I know it's time for a change. When I am just a little out of balance everything starts to fall apart, and then I lose sleep at night even when there are no rats in the furnace.

.

Chapter 21
AROUND THE TABLE

I am privileged to do my pastoring along rural lanes and countryside and in quaint villages and small towns. My parish is a beautiful one. This time of the year the gentle hills and glens of Knox County are ribboned with ripening crops and rich with the colors of autumn.

Robert Frost wrote of "being versed in country things"; that is an ambition of mine. I love the old places in the country best—bank barns and big family homes back long, tree-lined lanes. I like houses with character and history, not cookie-cutter track-houses but unique homes with their own personalities and atmospheres. I like houses that look like they have stories to tell.

Our good neighbors, the Wheelers, have a home like that. It is nestled in a ravine back a quarter-mile lane in the middle of a one hundred-acre farm. On the back porch is a sturdy, wrought iron, triangular dinner bell.

I can imagine little children, grimy with play, running for the house at the sound of that bell. Their daddy, coming in from the field, hangs his cap on a hook inside the back porch and rolls up his sleeves. He scrubs for dinner then cups his hands to drink the cold water. He takes his place at the head of the table and with all the family holding hands bows his head and says a humble, sincere prayer of thanksgiving. The aroma of good food and coffee is in the air. The home is marked by the bounty of God.

We don't live at the end of a lane in a spacious farmhouse. We don't have a dinner bell and I don't work in the fields, but there are a couple things about this little scenario that we have been able to duplicate.

Every time we sit down to eat as a family, we join hands around a beautiful, solid oak, dining room table. The big table should be in our family for generations. It was custom-built by an Amish man from Walnut Creek named Sam Mast. We waited months for it to be finished. On August 10, 1990, we all loaded in the van and drove up through Holmes County to get it. It was a big family event.

I think if I tell you the story behind how we got that table and what we plan to do with it you will be strengthened in your resolve to have a godly home.

It is an unusual story involving the Amish and the Japanese, Athens and Tokyo, a lady who calls herself Anne, a niece of Sam and his cousin, the Honda Motor Company, and Disney World.

The table didn't cost me a penny. Lois doesn't have a job but she paid for it. One day, looking for an outlet for some homemade craft items, Lois called a friend named Joanna (who calls herself Anne). Anne put her in touch with a lady from Athens (Ohio) who had a contract with the Honda Motor Company to supply American-made dolls for a promotion sponsored by Disney World in Tokyo. Lois called the lady from Athens, who told her she would buy all the dolls she could make. There was, however, a stipulation. The deadline for the order was less than a week away.

We set a goal to make sixty dolls in three days. The whole family worked together. The oldest children stuffed doll arms and legs and torsos with polyester batting. I stuffed and stitched doll pantaloons. Lois did the rest. I helped with meals. We stayed up all night most of two nights. I carefully maintained my office hours and took care of my calls and study and meetings and administrative duties, but when the deadline came we delivered on our end of the bargain. Thirty days later a check for over six hundred dollars arrived in the mail.

We went shopping for a table. The retail stores wanted more than we could afford but I could tell the tables were made locally. Not knowing how to locate the Amish man who made the tables, I stopped an Amish lady on the street in Sugar Creek and asked if she knew anyone who built custom furniture. She said; "Oh, yes, my cousin, Sam Mast does. He lives near Mount Hope."

We drove to Mount Hope. At a little country store we stopped again. I asked the girl at the counter if she knew where Sam Mast lived. From the middle aisle of the store a voice said, "Sam Mast is my uncle," and she told us how to find his house.

We drove to his home and described the table we wanted. We wanted solid oak, five legs, simple and sturdy. We wanted bow-back chairs on the ends and benches on the sides. We wanted a light finish. We wanted five leaves so it would open to ten feet. We held our breath as he looked up the price. Altogether it came to six hundred dollars!

In a way, the table represents the heart of our home.

It is large in hopes that God will bless us with enough children to go around it. *". . . Like olive plants all around your table" (Psalm 128:3).*

It is beautiful to remind us that a truly godly family is a thing of great beauty and powerfully attracts others to the Christian faith. (We want to use it to welcome others to our home and to our faith.)

It is simple to encourage us to remember that function is primary.

It is strong to inspire us to bear up under the weight of the pressures that a family must endure.

It is flexible. The leaves may be added when the family is large or there are many guests. But there will be a day, all too soon, when we won't need all the leaves and we must use these short days to prepare the children to gather their own families around tables of their own. We want to

raise them in such a way that they will always long to return and that returning will remind them that faith and family are the most important things in life.

It is the product of hard work.

It is the product of working together.

Some families rarely have a family meal together. They just "graze" all day. They wander from the fridge to the microwave then park it in the living room to stare at the big electronic "eye." Not us. We gather around a beautiful oak table every night.

Chapter 22
PARSHALLVILLE MILL

Here in Michigan on autumn days people like to drive the back roads and take in the color. During an excursion like that you want to keep your eyes open for apple orchards and cider mills. For the last three years or so we have made a family event of visiting the Parshallville Mill.

At the Parshallville Mill they have fresh apple cider and diet-wrecker cinnamon-sugar donuts. There is an old grist mill there and a dam and water running over rocks reflecting the bright colors of the leaves. There are a couple footbridges and the proprietor has a nicely restored old Ford 9-N that brings back sweet memories of my grandpa's farm in Licking County, Ohio. If you catch them on a slow day they are always eager to talk about cider-making or the history of the mill or area. It's close enough to be convenient and far enough to be an event.

Sometimes our little family outings just don't work. They get rained out, or the kids fuss, or the parents fuss, or schedule conflicts choke them out, or the budget gets in the way, but they are important. They take effort but they are worth it.

I consider it a dad's duty to arrange family memories. That requires planning, sacrifice, investment, and selfless energy. Making memories is serious business, but it's the kind of thing that makes kids want to hang around home and listen to Mom and Dad and learn to love and value what Mom and Dad love and value. Sometimes truth just goes down a lot better with cider and donuts under a flaming maple on a crisp autumn day beside a gurgling stream. I think that's the way Jesus did it. When Jesus re-enlisted Peter after his denial, Jesus didn't invite him to a lecture. He fixed Peter breakfast beside the lake at sunrise. He knew what he was doing.

I just think if our families aren't fun they are not worthy of the name "Christian." If there is no joy in our homes there is no evidence of the Spirit's presence, because the fruit of the Spirit is joy. Where families lack joy, they lack the magnetic power that draws children to the One who was anointed with the oil of gladness above his fellows. Jesus was a joyful, happy man. (See the first chapter of the epistle to the Hebrews, verse nine.)

Recently I drove into Sugar Creek, Ohio. I stopped for a cup of coffee at a spot that overlooks the little hamlet. There is an old restored railroad there. Looking on it my mind traveled back about fifteen years to a snapshot I cherish of four little chubby-faced children on that train on that day. Before Christmas those children will be 25, 22, 21, and 19 years old. One is a married man now. I don't know how long it will be before the others will make their way out into the world.

As the memories flooded back, my heart was tender with happiness for the joy we had together and eager for the times we will have in the future. I was glad, so glad, that I took the time and spent the money and set aside televised sports and selfish hobbies to spend time with the children and with Lois. As I drove through Sugar Creek and Charm and Walnut Creek and Berlin and Farmerstown and the gentle hills between them, I was glad that I had indulged myself in family events through the years.

I worshiped the Lord that afternoon and spent some tender, tearful moments with him, talking out loud to the Lord, thanking him for the sweetness of family memories and family affection, pleading with him to never let my heart stray from my home, family, wife, and children into foolish, selfish things that won't matter in a few years.

Chapter 23
CREATIVE PARENTING

When I was a boy the death sentence was to have to go to bed without a "treat." To call what we ate before we went to bed at night a "treat" is a bit of a misnomer, because it was usually a full meal of leftovers. On Sunday night our "treat" was really our evening meal eaten after church. Sunday dinner was usually late because by the time we arrived home after talking with all the people we would eat late and then the evening service was upon us immediately after our naps. By the time we arrived home on Sunday evening we were ready to eat. I mean we were really ready to eat.

When I was hungry it was so hard for me not to misbehave. I'm still that way. You want to feed me or get out of the way. On the way home from church on Sunday nights I was always dangerously hungry. My parents tried all kinds of things to get me to behave, stopping just short of electric-shock therapy, capital punishment, or making me ride home on the roof rack. The last resort discipline, especially on Sunday evenings, was to have to go to bed without a treat.

One Sunday night in the car on the way home I pushed my parents just a bit too far and my dad dropped the gavel of judgment on me. "Kenny, that's it. You will go to bed without a treat tonight. Your mother and I have warned you over and over again."

A sudden sense of silent doom fell on the car. Even my brothers and sisters felt sympathy for me. No one spoke for the rest of the trip, and when we got home I was sent directly to my room. I climbed the narrow, wooden stairs like I was ascending the gallows and sat dejectedly on my bed without undressing, cursing my foolishness and listening to voices drifting up from below. I could smell the food and hear the noise of the plates and glasses, knives, forks, and spoons.

Then there was another noise. Someone was coming up the staircase. It was my dad. He stepped into the doorway with a plate of food in his hand. He handed the plate to me. He sat down in the chair by my small desk and watched me. After a few bites I saw Dad was not eating. I looked at him.

"Did you already eat, Dad?"

"Kenny, I told you that you couldn't eat before you go to bed but I couldn't stand the idea of you going to sleep without any food. I'm taking your punishment. I'll go to bed without food so you don't have to go to bed hungry. I love you."

I ate and we both cried.

Dad taught, modeled, and illustrated Christlike love and biblical truth to his children every day. He knew that it was important for me to learn to behave, even when I was hungry. But it was more important to him that I understand the Gospel. He wanted me to understand that Jesus took my punishment on Calvary. My dad is a creative man. I thank God for him. I want to be like him.

Chapter 24
LOGANSVILLE, OHIO

Get out a map of Ohio. Look in the middle of the
state. The big city there is Columbus. Now look slightly to
the left. Do you see Bellefontaine? Follow State Route 47
west out of town until you see a little dot in the highway
labeled Logansville.

I lived there for a while when I was a little boy. I think
I was about ten. My dad was the pastor of the little church
built on the highway.

I spent many lazy afternoons riding my red balloon-
tire bike and exploring creeks. I dressed like Opie Taylor. I
wore Levi's every day with black sneakers (Red Ball Jets, as
I recall). I was never without a red wool ball cap tilted
back on my head. The sun would bleach the bangs of my
already blonde hair. I wore T-shirts with horizontal stripes.
That was before writing on T-shirts became popular.

One afternoon, overcome with boredom, I wandered
into my dad's study and asked him if he would help me
build a tree fort. He said no. "The trees aren't ours. This is a
parsonage. The people of the church may not want us to

build a tree house." I wasn't sure I liked being a pastor's kid. I went outside and nursed my wounds under a tree.

About ten minutes later I heard my dad whistling and looked up to see him coming across the yard. He wore a dress shirt and tie every day no matter what he was doing. But he had pulled cover-alls over his dress clothes and he had his tool box and some boards." Go get the ladder," he called. "We're going to build a tree house."

An hour later I was sitting on a board up in the crotch of a tree feeling a little like one of the Hardy boys. Dad rigged up a bucket and pulley so I could get things up in the tree. Sometimes Mom let me eat my lunch up there. From my post in the tree I could look down on life in the little crossroad village where we lived.

A mentor of my dad's at the time was an evangelist named John R. Rice. Dad said when John R. Rice was a boy he had a special place to be alone with the Lord. Dad said, "This can be your special place to be with the Lord. You can read your Bible here and pray." I loved that tree house and spent hours on my shady perch on summer days. We moved away one day, but I remembered it as one of the best places we lived growing up.

Many years later we came back to an area an hour or so south of Logansville. I worked about twenty miles north of where we lived. It was a third-shift job working all night with a crew of lewd, loud reprobates. They talked filth continually and played wretched music all night every night over a cheap PA system. Every night I worked with a knot in my stomach. It's hard for me to remember ever being more discouraged.

One night I took an hour off for lunch and got in my car and began to drive. I drove east in the night until descending into a little sleeping village. It must have been two or three o'clock in the morning. I found the house I remembered. I turned my little Volkswagen onto the street beside the house. I parked and shut off the engine. I sat in silence for a few minutes and looked up into an old maple tree. The boards were gone but the tree still stood in the corner of the yard.

After a few minutes I started the car up and went back to work. I've never been back. It's been over twenty years. It is one of the pleasant places I visit in my mind sometimes when I have been around too many reprobates and I've had to listen to too much loud music and my stomach is in knots.

If you have a little boy in your life, do something with him. Build something or go somewhere or take a walk and just be together. Someday you will consider it a great investment. Years from now when things get hard for him he will need some pleasant places to visit in his mind.

Chapter 25
THE HAND ON MY SHOULDER

When I was about twelve my dad, grandfather, and I joined some men from the church to visit the county jail. It was a tough place to conduct a service. Dad and Grandpa gave their testimonies and preached. Others sang and testified. They had to sing their songs and shout their messages through a small hole in a huge metal door.

Because the inmates were out of sight they were especially abusive. They shouted and swore and created as much havoc as possible. The men from the church were stalwarts. They were not going to tuck their tails and run just because of a little verbal opposition.

I stood and watched and listened. After most of the men had tried to testify or sing or read Scripture, Dad turned to me and said, "Why don't you give your testimony, Buddy."

My heart began to pound but I stepped up to the door. Dad said, "Speak right up clearly,

Buddy," and I launched into my testimony. I don't remember how long I spoke. I do remember two things very clearly. One was that the abusive language didn't stop.

The other thing I remember well is the feeling of my father's hand on my shoulder gently patting me the whole time I talked. He quietly whispered encouragements to me as I spoke." Good job, son. Keep going. That's right. Good. Good job." All the time I spoke he patted me gently on the shoulder.

It has been over thirty years and I have preached hundreds of times in scores of places, but I never preach without a subconscious sense of my father's hand on my shoulder.

Twice the Heavenly Father said similar things about his Son, the Lord Jesus. Once he said, "This is my beloved son in whom I am well pleased." On another occasion he said, "This is my beloved son, hear ye him." These divine affirmations were accompanied with miraculous signs. They were clearly symbolic and significant.

I'm not sure I understand all the significance of these occasions, but I know it is important to affirm our sons and daughters. I know their spirits are thirsty for it. There is great enduring power in the quiet, steady affirmation of a father to his son. You may not think it is important, but our sons and daughters long for this paternal approval.

When I'm with my children I want them to know that I love them. I want them to know I am pleased with them. I want them to know that I am eager to hear them and eager for others to hear them. I believe they have something to say.

I like to believe that, long after I am gone, my sons and daughters will hear my voice in a quiet place in their soul. I like to think they will see my smile. I like to think they will feel my hand on their shoulder.

Chapter 26
TRIBUTE TO MY DAD

You probably don't know my dad. He doesn't have a radio program. He's not a published author. He doesn't oversee a large staff. He's never been the keynote speaker at the conference. He's always been a full-time pastor but he has often also been a full-time schoolteacher or Christian school principal or even church custodian at the same time.

His specialty has been new church plants or recovery works. Over the years he's been attracted to churches that don't interest other men. He has always run his own bulletin—years of that on mimeograph machines, which should qualify him for a special crown. He does his own building maintenance. He watches the thermostat on the hot water heater and the thermometer in the church building during the week in order to be a good steward of God's money. He mows the lawn in the summer, rakes the leaves in the fall, and clears the snow in the winter.

He always does yard work in a tie, so he can quickly get to the jail or the hospital or the home of last week's visitor. I've been with him dozens of times when he has gone miles out of his way to get a carload of children who were not welcome at other churches. He is a tenderhearted man with a special interest in the unlovely. I've been with him on calls where he doubled as a plumber or auto mechanic. Wherever he has gone, he has served faithfully with integrity and diligence and he has made a mark. The mark has been modest, but eternal.

Observing my dad over the years has forced me to carefully evaluate what it means to be a successful man. In the world, if a man has a combination of wealth, strength, athletic ability, sexual attractiveness, position, respect, power, and influence—if he has the right toys and the right image—he is considered successful.

Many men have an insatiable lust for success. They are driven to achieve it. They thirst for its rewards. They fantasize about it. They sacrifice for it. Millions will sacrifice their family, their integrity, their leisure, their health, and their peace of mind just for a taste of the coveted nectar of success.

There are many, however, who cannot seem to put all the pieces together. These men sometimes fake it. They try to surround themselves with the accoutrements of success. They borrow to buy impressive wardrobes. They live beyond their means. They swagger and brag in a kind of pitiful bravado. They sit at the feet of motivational hucksters and pop-psychology gurus, hoping to find the right combination of factors that will catapult them to the pinnacle of personal success.

There are casualties in this war for success; men lie wounded on the battlefield like so much twisted, smoldering wreckage. For every man who dons the decorations of the war hero and marches in the parade of popular adulation, there are a thousand who join the grisly carnage of failure. These men consider themselves worthless, inconsequential, "also-rans," rejects on the scrap heap of humanity. They curse their fate and become hostile, or they just plod on through life with a spirit of pitiful resignation.

But there are thousands upon thousands of men who have achieved success who completely break the conventional mold. These are men who seem to be playing the game of life by an entirely different set of rules, and they are winning! They are not necessarily handsome. Few of them have acquired wealth. They are not usually athletic or even in particularly good physical condition. They are certainly not in envied positions of power.

They do not jet around the country or command hearings with important people. They do not boast of great sexual conquests. They usually live in obscurity. They may have very limited abilities. They are not all highly intelligent. These men are successful, but they will never make the cover of a magazine or be featured in television interviews. Their achievements are modest. They will live and die unknown beyond their immediate circle of family and friends, but they will taste the sweet fruit of success.

A successful man has a certain spiritual vitality. He has cultivated his inner man to the point that there is an obvious spiritual radiance about him. He seems to live life on a higher plane than most others. He has a deep, resonant purposefulness about him. His energies and schedule, his conversation and use of money, seem to drive toward that purpose and work in harmony.

He is a man of integrity. He can be depended upon to consistently do what is right. He inspires trust and confidence in people who do not even know him well because his eyes are clear. Those who do get to know him are not disappointed, because he is what he appears to be.

- He is honest but not pseudo-pious.
- He is confident but not arrogant.
- He is meek but not vacillating.
- He is generous but not foolish.
- He is humorous but not frivolous.
- He is spiritual but not detached.
- He is firm but not abrasive.
- He is strong but not rough.
- He always gives more than he takes.

He fails, he sins, he has personal weaknesses and character defects, but he admits his failures, right his wrongs, and he is quick to seek forgiveness.

He is constantly working to develop his personal character. A successful man knows the love of his family. He has won the admiration of his wife and the affection of his children. His wife and children want to please him because he has devoted his life to serving them.

His home is in order. It is not without its share of sickness and disappointment, financial challenges and emotional cycles, misunderstandings and pressures, but he is able to bring an inner tranquility to it.

He is purposeful and proactive. He knows where he is going and what he needs to accomplish. He ruthlessly insists that every activity contributes to the overall goal.

Why is he successful? How did he achieve this profile? What is the principle that unifies all that he does? How does he avoid the dangerous, alluring traps that claim so many of his peers? How does he keep from being distracted by pleasures that seem innocent but damage his home, disappoint his friends, and destroy his soul?

His secret is that he is at one with God through the Lord Jesus Christ. He has exchanged his own will for the will of God. He has made the Word of God the continual meditation of his heart and the ways of God his consuming desire. And because of that, though the culture in which he lives may not recognize it, he is a successful man. That is consistent with the sweet promise of the first Psalm.

"He shall be like a tree planted by the rivers of water, that brings forth its fruit in its season, whose leaf also shall not wither; and whatever he does shall prosper" (Psalm 1:3).

My dad is like that. He's a foot soldier in the army of God. I've had four decades to consider what it means to be a successful man. I used to wonder if dad was one. The best way I know to summarize my conclusions is in the words of a lovely old song:

"Does the place you're called to labor
Seem so small and little known?
It is great if God is in it.
And He'll not forget his own.
Little is much when God is in it!
Labor not for wealth or fame.
There's a crown—and you can win it,
If you run in Jesus' Name."

That's a song that harmonizes with Peter's words: *"The elders who are among you I exhort, I who am a fellow elder and a witness of the sufferings of Christ, and also a partaker of the glory that will be revealed: Shepherd the flock of God which is among you, serving as overseers, not by compulsion but willingly, not for dishonest gain but eagerly; nor as being lords over those entrusted to you, but being examples to the flock; and when the Chief Shepherd appears, you will receive the crown of glory that does not fade away" (I Peter 5:1–4).*

Chapter 27
MOTHER

"Her children rise up and call her blessed..."
(Proverbs 31:28).

She dreamed of you from the time she was a little girl cradling a baby doll in her arms. She always saw you playing around the little cottage in her childhood dreams. She carried you in her body and you made her sick every morning for weeks and weeks. She bore you into the world through intense pain, but when she heard you cry and saw your wrinkled face she forgot all about it and wept tears of joy.

She fed you at her breast and her whole world revolved around you. She stole into your room at night just to watch you sleep and she was sure you were the most beautiful child on earth. She sat up through the night to bathe away the fever and at breakfast your dad said, "Sleep well, Honey?" oblivious to the all-night vigil. She somehow always knew when you needed her, even in the middle of the night, and she came to your room and changed your bedding and made sure you were warm and dry.

She covered your ears and gave you your coat and checked your homework and made you practice the piano and sat through all your ball games and recitals like they were the seventh game of the World Series and a debut at Carnegie Hall. She urged you to brush your teeth with words of wisdom like "be true to your teeth, or they will be false to you." She changed your diaper and cleaned up when you were sick and washed underwear no one else would touch without a chemical suit. And who do you think always cleaned the gunk out of the kitchen sink and bathtub drain?

She made sure you had the drumstick and your dad had the breast and acted like she preferred the wings. Her oatmeal cookies made you forget the beating you took from the neighborhood bully or the slow rate of greeting card sales.

She listened to you and didn't laugh when others would have mocked you. She believed in you when you didn't believe in yourself and prayed for you even when you didn't think you needed it. She made you think you could do things you were sure you couldn't do. She was tough enough to call your bluff and discipline you and give you a sense of boundaries and the security that comes with it. She spanked you when you needed it even when popular psychology and self-proclaimed talk-talk show experts advised "time outs." She knew when you needed a spanking or just a nap and she didn't always give you candy though she longed to indulge you.

She was always waiting when you came in late. When you complained about it, she pretended to be asleep the way you always did when you wanted her to carry you in from the car after a long trip.

She read the Bible to you and read the Bible in front of you and did what mothers have to do to make sure the family is faithful in church. She made your dad a much better man than he ever would have been without her and probably covered for some of his failures too.

She mended clothes as a labor of love and it broke her heart to see how quickly you grew out of them. She knew you were only loaned to her from God and soon the house would fall silent again. She washed mountains of dishes and truckloads of laundry. She put up food on the hottest summer days and didn't complain.

Her most sincere prayers were the ones she sent heavenward in gratitude for you. She filled your home with fragrance and beauty and music, the smell of her perfume and fresh-cut flowers, bacon for breakfast and Sunday roast.

Her eyes were bright and happy and full of life. She wept though, wept and worried a thousand times for you when no one ever knew.

She rose early on holidays so you could enjoy a festive meal and an enduring memory. She planned for days and worked for hours so that in a few minutes you could gulp it down and go watch football. You didn't always thank her or help her with the dishes, but those meals have been a cherished memory for years. She baked you special treats just to watch you eat them. Something inside made her happier the more you ate.

She wore old dresses so you could have a new ball glove. She skipped vacations and second honeymoons so you could go to camp. She limited expenses for her hobbies so you could get your band instrument. She was happy with last year's fashion so you could have this year's tennis shoes.

She didn't abandon the family when your dad was insensitive to her needs. She took the blame for your failures and stood back and let your dad have the glory for your successes.

And having done all these things and a thousand others that make *mother* a sacred word, she still felt she wasn't the mother she should have been.

Chapter 28
LUNCH HOUR IN UTICA

If my life were a movie I would fast-forward through junior high. My junior high years were painful. Like every junior high kid, I was struggling toward manhood, and wrestling with who I was and how I would make my mark in life. But I was sure I was alone with these strange feelings.

I was trying and failing in a number of things. I wanted to excel in athletics but had not yet figured out that that would never happen. I wasn't academic enough to spell *academic*. (I'm a little surprised right now that I was able to spell that without the aid of my nifty little Microsoft Word spell checker.) I was trying to gain a spot in the pecking order as a new kid in school, all the while suffering the rejection of most of my peers, being cut from the basketball team, failing to play football that I so wanted to play. It was a time of questioning how girls saw me and wanting so much to be loved and accepted. To be loved and accepted seemed to me at the time something I could never in all my life achieve.

During that time I would go through the cafeteria line and eat alone feeling unloved and unnoticed. As spring came one day I was starting out the door and complaining that I had no one to eat with.

Mom said to me, "If you want you can come home for lunch." That day when lunch came it was a beautiful spring day in the hills of central Ohio. The bell rang at noon and I bolted from the school and ran across the little village home to eat. I wondered if my mom would remember. When I came through the door Mom was getting a little chicken pot pie out of the oven for me. It was a very humble lunch. It was just one of those four-for-a-dollar pot pies with little diced pieces of chicken, frozen peas, and carrots in some chicken gravy.

Mom set a cloth napkin beside my plate at the end of the table just beneath the window. I sat at our humble kitchen table in the tiny white house we rented on Maple Street in Utica. Mom listened to me while I talked about whatever was on my mind. In about fifteen minutes my time was up and I sprinted back to school.

That was in about 1972, over thirty-five years ago. My mom at the time was in her early thirties. She seemed so old to me then. Thirty-year-olds seem like children to me now. She sat across the table for about fifteen minutes and looked at me and listened to me and three and a half decades later I remember those times with fondness. She just paid attention to me. It's a powerful thing to pay attention to people.

Now you know a little more about how I see home. Home is a place where you don't have to sit alone and eat. Home is a place where people don't ignore you and avoid you. Home is a place where it doesn't really matter that much what's on the menu. Simple things are sweet to the taste in an atmosphere of love and security and acceptance. Moms are people who listen to you when no one else is interested. Moms don't ever think the small, mundane things you do don't matter. Moms don't laugh at your dreams. Good moms pay attention. Great moms fix you something warm to eat and pay attention.

I'm not sure what was happening at the time, but I know those little chicken pot pies were not worthy of a breathless dash across town. With the clarity of vision that the years bring, I now know that my soul needed a friendly place of warm acceptance for a few minutes a day. I didn't need my stomach filled as much as I needed my emotional fuel tank refilled. And refueling an emotional fuel tank is a good mother's specialty.

Chapter 29
CUTAWAY

They say it's good for a swimming pool to be agitated regularly. I guess it keeps mold and scum from growing in the water. Pool agitation is one of the Pierpont family's hidden talents. Few families do it better. There are ten of us in our family and you should see us boil the water.

If you ever go away for a week and you need someone to come over every day and agitate your pool, look no further. We are the family you are looking for. If you negotiate wisely you may even qualify for a discount. Some have gotten a week of free lawn care out of the deal, even.

A couple summers ago some friends in our church gave us their garage door opener and left us with detailed instructions to agitate their pool. We took the responsibility with appropriate gravity and dutifully made our way down there every day to stir the water.

One evening I was treading water and my then seventeen-year-old-son was toeing the end of the diving board. I asked him, "Kyle, have you ever done a cutaway?"

"No," he answered. "How do you do it?"

"Simple," I said. "Just stand backward, jump out toward the center of the pool, tuck your upper body under, and go in head first."

He tried it two or three times awkwardly and then on about the third time he tucked and cut nicely into the water.

"Not bad, Kyle. I think you got it. Keep working on it."

The whole time I was treading water and working on my wrinkles. He turned to me and said, "Show me how it's done, Dad."

I said, "Are you kidding? I never have been able to do that dive." He stared at me with surprise. I chuckled to myself that I was able to teach my son to do something that I have never been able to do myself.

It is not the first time that has happened, and I pray it will not be the last. There are some goals a young man can achieve that have eluded his father, if he can just stand on his father's shoulders. There are many mistakes I have made that my children don't need to repeat.

I consider it consolation for falling short of some goals to be able to instruct and encourage my children to reach levels of competence beyond me. There are physical feats, social graces, athletic achievements, and spiritual accomplishments they will enjoy that I only dreamed about. That is a large part of the reward of parenting. It's a kind of consolation to enjoy while I am working on my cutaway.

(I am pleased to report that at the encouragement of my family, on the evening of June 13 at about 8:30 p. m. I pulled off my first cutaway. It was a little awkward but I did it, and it took me only forty-two years.)

Chapter 30
LIKE WILLOWS BY THE WATER

Years ago God planted a seed of vision in my heart for a godly family. Since then I have continually asked God to help me raise a family that would stir the hearts of others to embrace the ways of God.

A peaceful family in chaotic times

A loyal family in factious times

A diligent family in slothful times

A harmonious family in discordant times

A humble family in haughty times

A loving family in self-centered times

A worshipful family in irreverent times

An obedient family in rebellious times

A wise family in foolish times

A Bible-loving family in Bible-rejecting times

An honest family in defiled times

A simple family in complex times

A giving family in selfish times

A content family in materialistic times

A gentle family in violent times

The world we live in is very hostile to that vision. The jarring reality is that vision alone will not produce a beautiful, well-tended garden. Weeds will overcome the plants and choke off any possibility of fruitfulness if I am not unmerciful in attacking them. The family of my vision will have to be led by a father who rises with the sun every day to seek the character of the Lord Jesus Christ.

I remember a summer evening a few years ago. We spent the evening with close friends. Fireflies hovered over the moistening lawn. Children laughed and danced and played barefoot in the grass. We talked about things that were sacred to us and we ate cold, sweet watermelon. As I enjoyed the treat it occurred to me that a piece of melon like that was nothing less than a miracle of God's creation.

Melons like that don't just show up in your garden one day voluntarily. They have to be planted and cultivated, watered and tended, harvested and transported with watchful care from the seed to the roadside stand. Our families will demand nothing less if we hope to achieve even a fraction of our God-given goals for them.

When I need to restore my vision for a godly family I keep my heart open for the family promises of the Bible. They are everywhere. An example would be the promise of Isaiah 44:3-4: *"For I will pour water on him who is thirsty, and floods on the dry ground; I will pour My Spirit on your descendants, and My blessing on your offspring; They will spring up among the grass like willows by the watercourses."*

By God's sustaining grace I will never give up my highest vision for the family God has entrusted to me. I pray that God will remind me of that vision every time I pillow my head and every time birdsongs herald the arrival of a new day.

Chapter 31
HELP WITH BIG DECISIONS

A couple years ago I began to notice that my precious oldest daughter was moving from pretty little girl to beautiful young woman. Her name is Holly and we have an agreement. I get to help her find a husband when the time comes. She doesn't want to make the decision alone. She thinks her mother and I have experience and objectivity that will help her evaluate potential mates when opportunities arise.

One day that summer it was unusually hot so we loaded up the van and headed for the beach. We lived about thirty minutes from Lake Michigan, but the beach we wanted to visit was about an hour and a half away. By the time we got there we were hot and the children were irritable. There were seven of them that summer—children, that is.

Arriving at the lake we parked our car under shade trees. We had to walk about 150 yards to the beach. It was a hot, humid walk. Our parking place was high above the lake and we had to walk through trees that obscured our view of the water. At the same time the huge body of blue water burst into view, a cool, strong, steady wind hit us in the face. Both the view and the breeze were refreshing and breathtaking. We all climbed down the long steps that descended to the beach and spent the rest of the day in the clear, refreshing water.

It was one of those family days that you can't fully plan or orchestrate but by evening we knew that we were tucking a sweet memory into the scrapbook of our hearts. We ate there (sandwiches, what else) and finally and regretfully the sun began to sink lower and lower toward the straight line where the water met the sky in the west.

Little driftwood fires began to flare up along the beach as the evening turned toward nighttime. Stars began to appear. As the sun was setting I saw Holly standing with her toes at the edge of the water, watching the sunset. I joined her there, taking her hand in mine. "Someday, Holly, when you're married, you and your husband can come to a beautiful place like this. Won't that be romantic?" I said.

"Oh, yes," she said and smiled.

"And you know what, Holly?" I said. "I hope your husband and I will be best friends." The words she said next that night on the beach are words I will treasure in my heart for years.

She looked at me with the beautiful dark brown eyes that she got from her mother and said, "Oh, you will be good friends, Dad. You're going to pick him."

One Christmas my wife and I found a special gift for Holly that would express our love for her and convey a special meaning whenever she looked at it. It was a beautiful little ring with two hearts and two diamonds. It is a symbol of the covenant that we have between us.

It is sobering to realize that she is depending on me to help her make such an important decision. I think it keeps us close. She is looking to me for wisdom and I am on my knees looking to my Heavenly Father. It's one of the things that keep me close to him.

Chapter 32
THE LOVE PEOPLE CRAVE

My dad was a very, very good dad to me when I was growing up. Still is. I loved him deeply and I was eight or ten years old before I could imagine that he ever did anything wrong.

I loved spending time with my dad but I had three big problems. First, my dad was a seminary student. Second, my dad was a pastor. Third, my dad was a full-time second-shift factory worker.

Mom was tucking me into bed one night when I asked her to have Dad come in and kiss me good night when he got home from work. She promised to tell him. I decided to stay awake until he came in. I tried with all my might to stay awake but soon I was sleeping.

When I woke up it was in the middle of the night. I called out to my mom. "Mom . . . Mom . . . Mom? MOOOOOOMMMM!"

"What, Kenny?"

"You said you were gonna have Dad kiss me good night when he got home from work."

"He did, Kenny, but you were asleep."

"I wanted to be awake."

I cried and Mom said, "Go to sleep, Kenny. Your dad is tired."

I didn't.

The next voice I heard was my dad's voice.

"Kenny, I said good night to you when I came in. Now go to sleep."

I didn't.

"Come here, Kenny."

I went into my parents' room. Poor Dad must have been exhausted from a long week of classes and a full-time second-shift factory job." Son, I love you. Here, let me hug you." He did. I still wasn't happy. I continued to cry and complain that he should have awakened me when he got in. That was the agreement as I had understood it. I couldn't put the injustice to rest, and I wouldn't let my parents get any rest until they did.

Finally, Dad said, "Kenny, if you don't go and get in bed and go to sleep now, I am going to have to spank you." I didn't. Finally Dad drew back his hand in the darkness to swat me on the bottom, but when he did his arm hit the table beside the bed and the table hit the window and the window broke. It didn't crack; it shattered. And it wasn't spring; it was winter. And we didn't live in Miami; we lived in Grand Rapids, Michigan.

For the first time since I had woken up I was quiet. I stepped back to see what Dad would do. He turned on the light, wearily got out of bed, and found some cardboard and duct tape to cover the broken pane until morning.

Three-quarters of an hour later we were all tucked back in our warm beds.

The next day was a Saturday. I watched my dad pick up the broken glass from the snow beneath the window. He spent a good part of the morning measuring the window, getting a pane of glass from the hardware, and putting it in place. As I watched I thought to myself, "Wouldn't it have been a lot easier to just get up and come in my room and kiss me good night?"

The way I see it, it's a lot easier just to give people the love they crave than it is to clean up the mess when you don't.

Chapter 33
IN CASE YOU EVER FORGET

My Grandpa Shipley was a man of few words, but they were usually well-chosen ones.

When we prepared to leave Grandma and Grandpa's little house after a visit, the whole family would form a circle and hold hands and Grandpa would pray—in a few well-chosen words. The last thing you heard before you went down the steps and through the breezeway was his little life motto:"Remember whose you are."

His motto had a double meaning. He always wanted you to remember that you belonged to the Lord and that you belonged to him too. I think it also served as a gentle reminder to live up to your name and maintain a good testimony for Christ. He had the initials *RWYA* printed on pencils and cards as a testimony to his family, friends, and customers.

In the last few months of Grandma's she life would often say, "Grandpa just isn't Grandpa."

He would forget so much. He struggled to put a complete sentence together. Sometimes he forgot the names of his loved ones. The confusion that clouded his mind frustrated him.

He loved the song "Overshadowed." It always moved him to tears and he requested it whenever he got a chance but in the last few months of his life he didn't even register recognition when it was played for him. Toward the end of his life his daughter, my Aunt Sue, asked him, "Daddy, do you remember whose you are?" He smiled immediately and said, "I'm the Lord's."

When you think about it, it really doesn't matter what you forget as long as you . . . Remember Whose You Are.

Chapter 34
MY BLUE SPORT COAT

When I was a little boy, my hair was white blonde. In the summer, the sun would bleach it even whiter and I spent a lot of time out of doors on account of my parents liked the peace and quiet.

My mom loved to sew and she could create a dress in a day. (I'm sure there were many times my mom could cut out a dress and sew it and alter it to fit in less time than it took to pick a pattern and choose the fabrics. I was a reluctant member of the pattern-picking-fabric-choosing party more times than I care to recall.)

One spring, Mom decided I needed a new sport coat for Easter Sunday. Light blue was my "season." I've seen pictures of this and I did look very dapper. I was an exceptionally cute kid. This fact has been confirmed by a number of impartial, non-related people. I was especially cute in this light blue sport coat.

At the time, Dad was pioneering a church in the village of Wayland, Michigan. The church was meeting in the basement of the post office. Through the week, the basement room was used as a pool hall. We would come in early Sunday morning and scoot the pool tables to the back of the room, sweep up the cigarette butts, and set up folding chairs. Dad had a light metal lectern that he used for a pulpit. Mom accompanied the congregational singing on the piano. They made an impressive team. Easter Sunday in 1963, I would have been five years old. We would celebrate next Easter in a new building, a small, red brick colonial out across Interstate 131.

At the close of the message that morning, I received a call from nature at the precise time Dad began to draw the net and Mom's services were required to accompany the invitation. To get to the little boys' room, you had to go down the aisle to the front and walk past the preacher and down a little hallway. A calling only I understood propelled me forward that morning.

Too late I discovered that the little boys' room was not adequately supplied with the necessary "paperwork." Needless to say, by the time my mom looked in on me, I was a mess. My blue sport coat was a mess. I could immediately tell by the look on my mom's face that I had done the wrong thing. She just said, "Oh, Kenny," closed the door, and walked away.

A long time passed, it seemed to me. Finally Mom came back. I suppose she considered just leaving me there and going home, but her maternal instincts must have taken over and she came back, cleaned me up, and kept me. I don't think I ever wore the jacket again.

I wish this was the only mess I had ever made of things. I'm afraid it's not. Some of my messes have embarrassed my family, brought pain to ones I love, and grieved my Heavenly Father. Thank God, in spite of them all, he has chosen to clean me up and keep me. He's a good Father. He throws away the garments stained with sin and he cleans up the boy and keeps him. I will always love him for that!

"The Lord is merciful and gracious, slow to anger, and abounding in mercy. He will not always strive with us, nor will He keep His anger forever. He has not dealt with us according to our sins, nor punished us according to our iniquities. For as the heavens are high above the earth, so great is His mercy toward those who fear Him; As far as the east is from the west, so far has He removed our transgressions from us. As a father pities his children, so the Lord pities those who fear Him. For He knows our frame; He remembers that we are dust" (Psalm 103:8–14).

Chapter 35
THE FATHER'S ALL-SEEING EYE

If I had a twenty-dollar bill for every time I have eaten at the "golden arches" I would have enough money to buy my own franchise. If cheeseburgers are bad for you, my days are numbered. I'm probably about half cheeseburger myself. I can tell you our family's MacOrder from memory.

One day three-year-old Danny and I were in line after having dinner, thinking about a little post-meal snack. The line was long, I was tired, and most of the family had already gone to the van. After a long wait I decided that I would skip the after-meal snack and save my money. I headed for the door. At the door I turned to notice that Daniel had not seen me leave and he was standing alone in a crowd of strangers, probably trying to decide between chocolate and vanilla.

Rather than calling to him right away, I thought I would just watch him for awhile.

For the longest time he stood dutifully in line. Finally, I saw him turn and look at the people standing around him. He didn't recognize any of the pants and shoes around him so his little head went up and he began to search the faces of the strangers standing nearby.

Panic set in and he began to turn quickly from side to side with a little look of desperation on his face. My heart melted and I called out, "Danny, over here." A look of relief came to his eyes as soon as he heard my voice, and when he turned and saw me by the door he broke into a sweet, broad, toothless grin and sprinted toward me.

For just a moment he had searched for me, and he couldn't see me, but there was never even a fraction of a second that I took my eyes off him.

There have been times in my life when I thought God was missing. I couldn't find him. I felt panic rise in my heart and I felt abandoned and alone, but there never was a time when my Heavenly Father lost sight of me.

"He Himself has said,'I will never leave you nor forsake you' " (Hebrews 13:5). "Where can I go from Your Spirit? or where can I flee fromYour presence? If I ascend into heaven,You are there; if I make my bed in hell, behold,You are there. If I take the wings of the morning, and dwell in the uttermost parts of the sea, even there Your hand shall lead me, and Your right hand shall hold me. If I say, 'Surely the darkness shall fall on me,' even the night shall be light about me; Indeed, the darkness shall not hide from You, but the night shines as the day; the darkness and the light are both alike to You" (Psalm 139:7–12).

Chapter 36
I'M TOUGH, I'M TOUGH

Chuck was working with me at the little country church where I pastored at the time. He was just a little guy, about three. He left his books on the floor of my study and made his way to the restroom. He was gone a little too long, so I went to check on him. The restroom door often stuck at that time of the year, due to the humidity. I wanted to make sure he wasn't stuck.

As I approached the door I could hear him singing while he washed his hands. I decided to have a little fun with him. I held my foot against the door. In a minute I felt the weight of his little body pushing against the door. I didn't budge. Then I heard him say, "I'm tough, I'm tough." He must have backed up and run at the door, because there was a short interval of quiet and then a thud on the door. It didn't budge. Then at the top of his lungs he cried out desperately, "Daaaaaaaaaad."

The fear in his voice touched my heart and I quickly pulled open the door. We laughed. In that instant light fell on my heart. When I come up against a difficult problem I throw all my weight against it. I say, "I'm tough, I'm tough." Sometimes when I give it everything I have, I find that problems give way, but there are those times when every ounce of strength I can muster, every bit of creativity at my disposal, every talent I can apply leaves me helpless with my problem. Then I remember to cry out, "Daaaaaaaaaad," and my Heavenly Father's heart is stirred by the desperation of my cry and he comes to my rescue. The Father heart of God is tuned to hear my cry!

"The LORD is near to those who have a broken heart, and saves those such as have a contrite spirit" (Psalm 34:18).

"Call upon Me in the day of trouble; I will deliver you, and you shall glorify Me" (Psalm 50:15).

Chapter 37
JUST IN TIME

I almost didn't make it. I pushed all day to be ready to go at five. I would miss breaks and skip lunch and call in favors from others in the office. I had planned my route and I had timed it in my mind over and over again.

I would have to have good traffic and I would have to run down the stairs instead of waiting for the elevator. I would have to log off the phone, put away my work, close the office, and be out the door by three minutes after five. I didn't dare waste a minute. I could not allow myself to get involved in conversation with anyone.

The weather was clear. Looking out toward the outer-belt I could see traffic was moving along well. I would be just a little ahead of the main rush if I didn't get held up.

Things went flawlessly. I logged off, closed the office, grabbed my jacket and keys, and headed for the back stairwell. I ran through the parking lot to my car, jumped in, started the car, and headed out of the lot ahead of everyone else. I knifed my old Volvo into the flow of traffic and moved immediately into the fast lane and punched the gas, speeding immediately up to seventy-four miles an hour, and set the cruise. I tuned the radio to 640 AM to hear traffic reports. Everything was smooth. Everything now would depend on traffic and if the car would stay in overdrive. It would usually pop out of overdrive if it got too hot or if I had to take it out of gear. If I could leave it in gear and keep a steady pace, I could use the overdrive all the way home.

I loosened my tie and took a deep breath. There was a semi pulling into the fast lane ahead, passing another truck. I grumbled under my breath and tapped the brake to disengage the cruise control. I coasted up on the tail of the truck and waited until I could shoot around him. I carefully wove in and out of the other rush hour traffic as the subdivisions turned to farms.

Finally my exit came into view. I pulled off the interstate and onto State Route 95. There would be one stop in Chesterville unless I got the light and then eight miles to town. I hammered the little car and kept a sharp eye for the efficient Ohio State Highway Patrol. None were in sight. I darted around an elderly lady in a perfect old Chevy and shot around a tractor hauling a chisel plow. I gave it a little more gas and checked my watch: 5:56 p. m. "Oh, of all times I hope they are not ahead of schedule tonight."

I prayed again as I had done over and over again that day, wondering if God would answer the prayer of a man who is breaking the speed limit at the time.

I geared the car down at the edge of town. Now it was past six. I was late. I braked hard and turned left. There was no place to park. The crowd had gathered. At first I didn't see any familiar faces. I coasted to a stop in the grass and released my seat belt and jumped from the car. I sprinted to the fence and vaulted over.

There he stood, and he saw me the second I saw him. Our eyes met for a second and I thought a smile crossed his lips just for a second before he glared back at the batter, ground his heel in the rubber, and tossed the first pitch down the heart of the plate.

"Strike!" growled the umpire.

"Great pitch, Chuck. This guy is yours!" I shouted. "Now put him away, Buddy."

Beside me a pretty woman smiled and handed me a chili dog with relish and onions and a Diet Coke.

Chapter 38
BATTING A STRING

What does it take to make you happy? I think happiness depends more on what you do with what you have than it does on what you have. Let me give you an example.

Saturday night I needed the house to be quiet, and eight children can make a house a very noisy place. My week had been busy and the weekend was worse. I really needed to have some quiet study time and I didn't want to work at the church. I wanted to stay with the family, so I told them that if they wanted me to stay home they would have to be especially quiet so I could study. They all agreed.

I changed into comfortable clothes, arranged my workspace for undistracted study, and got down to business on the work. Suddenly my concentration was broken by a loud, repeated, banging sound. Over and over again whatever was causing the noise seemed to shake the whole house.

Not wanting to express anger or irritation, I called Hannah in and said, "Would you please go downstairs and ask whoever is making that loud noise to come and see me?" I said, "Ask them real nice, but tell them to come right away." She went away and the pounding noise continued to shake the whole house.

A few minutes later Hannah came back with a funny look on her face and said, "It's Mom making the noise. Do you want me to tell her to come up?"

"No, but what is she doing?" I asked.

"Oh, she's jumpin' on bubble wrap," Hannah answered.

That's what I mean when I say that happiness depends more on what you do with what you have than it does on what you have. Arranging perfect surroundings and accumulating expensive things will not guarantee satisfaction in life. My wife is a simple woman with a childlike love for life. It doesn't take much to make her happy or she wouldn't have put up with me for over two decades. You just have to get her out to Wal-Mart kinda regular, let her get to the mailbox first, and keep a fresh supply of bubble wrap on hand.

Take a lesson from my wife. Don't be so hard to please. And cultivate the ability to find joy in simple things. Like a boy kicking a can or a kitten batting a string.

Chapter 39
TRAIL HIKE

A trail hike was the perfect order of the day. The boys were excited about the idea. It would be a good workout, and it would be good to be together. We planned to leave immediately after lunch. I noticed that Daniel, who will be ten in November, and Wes, who will be seven in December, scrambled for their gear. They had spent the morning poring over outdoor outfitter catalogs looking at sophisticated equipment that would be sufficient to thru-hike the Appalachian Trail. I thought back over the years to the hours I had spent with my official Boy Scout handbook. I was disgusted to remember that I spent more time reading about nature than I spent experiencing it. That's when I said, "Guys, let's just use the daypacks we have and take a nice hike this afternoon."

They say the smallest deed is better than the grandest intention. The boys heartily agreed.

Immediately after dinner we made for the trailhead. Chuck joined us and led the expedition. He carried no pack. The little guys fell in on the trail ahead of me with their full daypacks, slouch hats complete with hand-tied flies hooked into the band, and Nalgene bottles filled with water. (Hydration is a life-and-death issue when you forge into the wild like this.) They soon found walking sticks. I laughed as I watched Wes lurching along the trail ahead of me struggling with all his gear. The fully loaded Nalgene bottle dangling from a loop on his pack had to equal a quarter of his total body weight and reached nearly to the ground. He shuffled along behind his brothers, careful not to drop behind. Not a syllable of complaint escaped his lips.

We hiked up some steep banks, through pine woods and across a meadow overlooking a pond. We climbed to the crest of a hill up an earthen stairway built into the hillside. Finally I asked Wes if I could carry the pack for a while. He smiled quietly and handed the thing to me. I noticed the compass hanging on a loop and a carabiner. (The compass, I suppose, so we wouldn't stray from the trail and find ourselves at the mercy of the elements. The carabiner would be useful if in our Herculean struggle for survival we had to scale a steep ascent and wanted to lash ourselves together for safety.)

The guys hiked quietly, trying to "leave no trace." The air was sweet with the scent of autumn. Goldenrod nodded yellow along the trail. Here and there a maple showed its color. In places, falling leaves streamed across the footpath overhead. Crows called out our location, giving us away. We crossed a footbridge over a stream that ran among small boulders. At one point we came to the edge of the wood overlooking acres of corn ripening in an undulating field. In the center of the field sat a pleasant farmhouse, barn, and silo.

I kept Wes's pack and finally asked him, "What's in the pack, Wes?"

"A calculator," he said. I thought I had misunderstood him. I thought maybe trail mix, some apples, or maybe even some jerky would be good things to put in the pack. Maybe he packed a field guide, field glasses, the writings of Thoreau, or the poems of Robert Frost or another of the nature poets. Any of these would have made sense, but Wes said, "A calculator." After forcing the boy to repeat himself as if he were shouting over the roar of a jet engine or the din of a factory or the rush of whitewater, I finally said; "Oh, a cal-cu-la-tor. . . ???"

"What else did you put in here, Wes?" "That's all." "It's kinda heavy, Buddy. Did you put some books in here too?" "No, just the calculator." He insisted the only thing the pack contained was a calculator. Then it hit me what he meant by calculator. He was talking about the huge desktop adding machine that had been underfoot at home for the last few weeks. It was complete with a grounded power cord and a roll of paper. I was trekking the wide outdoors with an adding machine in my backpack.

"Great," I thought. "If we find a handy power source I can stop and add up how many wild animals we scared off thundering though the woods hunched over like Piltdown man."

"Why did you put an adding machine in your pack?"

"I just wanted something in my pack," he said.

Kids are fun and full of surprises. I chuckle within every time of think of it, and I am reminded what a priceless thing it is to have a little boy to hike with.

It's better to live than waste your precious life watching other people pretend to live on television. There are people out there who want your love, and it's good to be alive. Get out and do something with the family. Spend time with the people who love you while you still can. Visit, ride bikes, stroll the beach, walk the dog, visit an orchard, get some pictures, go out for coffee and pie, walk the beach, go to church. If you can't think of anything better to do, throw an adding machine in a backpack and head off into the wild.

Chapter 40
RUNNING WHEN YOUR FATHER CALLS

Yesterday afternoon we met some friends for lunch. Looking up through the large plate-glass windows to the east, I could see Hope crossing the parking lot. Hope America is our three-year-old. Currently she is the baby of the family. I jumped from the chair and ran to the door. She was crossing the parking lot to get to her older sisters, who were leaving for a little shopping. I called to her as I ran out the door.

"Hope, come back here." She had been walking, but now that she thought I was going to keep her from going with her sisters, she turned and broke into a run. (It is a serious matter when you interfere with a woman of any age who is intent on shopping.)

"No, Hope. Stop!" I called out. She was in a full run. The words were barely from my mouth when her shoe caught on the ground. She fell face first on the asphalt. When I picked her up, she was still trying to wrestle free because she wanted to go with her sisters. Her knees were skinned but otherwise she was unhurt.

All I wanted to do was make sure she got safely across the parking lot and give her sisters a couple dollars for Starburst jelly beans. She just thought I was an old guy out to ruin her fun. I may be getting up in years, but I try to contribute to the fun whenever I can. The older she gets, I'm sure, the more she will know that to be true about me.

I suppose we all have a little of that in us though. We all have that tendency to doubt the goodness of the Father. We all fight the foolish impulse to turn and run away when he calls for us.

I gathered my baby into my arms and held her. Holding little Hope and wiping the tears from her face, I pressed a couple dollars into her hand for the jelly beans. I reminded myself that all the Father's gifts are good.

Today Lois told me that she read of a little boy who, when his father called to him, ran into traffic and was killed. Running when the Father calls can be a deadly habit. When you hear his voice, turn and run into his arms. He loves you, and his plans for you are better than you can imagine.

Hope is doing well. Her knees are pretty as ever. She brushed her teeth after the jelly beans and we have been working on teaching her to come quick when her daddy calls for her. When your Father calls, don't run. He is either protecting you from something bad, or he is trying to catch up to you with one of his blessings.

Chapter 41
MY FIRST BALL GLOVE

Every time we pass the Meijer Department Store on 28th Street in Grand Rapids, I say, "That's where I got my first ball glove." And the family groans. Sometimes I don't think they appreciate tradition like I do.

I get to Grand Rapids about three to five times a month to make hospital calls. A couple of times on a spring day I have gone out of my way to Francis Street and have driven slow past a house where we used to live. It was the house we lived in when Dad was in Vietnam. The people who live there now have widened the driveway I used to shovel for a dime. The new driveway is over a little strip of grass where my dad taught me to catch a baseball on a gentle evening years ago.

My dad was busy. He was a seminary student and worked at a grocery. He was not yet thirty. One spring evening he said, "You need your own ball glove." We got in the car and drove to Meijer's Thrifty Acres. I think it was the original Meijer Department Store, or at least an early one. I remember it well, because the roofline of the building forms an arch.

We walked back the aisles and chose a nice leather glove. Inside the palm the price was written with a marker pen: $5.95. On the way home Dad gave me a little talk about caring for the glove and breaking it in. He is a frugal man who takes care of things. He said, "If you take care of a good ball glove like that one, it will last you for years. Some people have one ball glove all their life." I took care of it and kept it for at least twenty-five years. It never wore out. Dad never had to buy me another glove.

After dinner my mom and sister did the dishes and Dad and I went out beside the driveway on a little strip of grass under a maple, and it was there he taught me to catch a baseball. I was an eager student and I will never be able to explain it but there is something about the exchange of a baseball between a father and son. I can still hear his instruction and encouragement. Sometimes he would get a little frustrated because I could not make the ball go where I wanted it to go. To encourage care, he sometimes had me chase the ball.

"Use your meat hand, son. Don't throw wild. Take your time with the throw. Aim for the glove. Okay, you run for that one, Buddy. Watch for cars, now. There you go. Try again. Nice throw. That one was almost too hot to handle."

Back and forth in a low arch the ball passes. Pop, pop. Pop, pop. Pop, pop. "Use your backhand, now. There you go. Good catch. You're getting the hang now."

The sun got low in the sky, and when we couldn't see to throw any more I went in and got ready for bed. We prayed and I put my new ball glove under my pillow. I put it under there because my dad bought it for me and I didn't want to lose it. I thought it might help break it in and I liked the smell of the leather.

It was a great ball glove. I used it all through Little League and even for softball in college. It must have been one of the best investments my dad ever made. How can you put a price tag on a memory like standing under the shade of a leafy maple on a summer evening and listening to the pop of the glove and smelling cut grass and leather and lilac all mixed together. I would still have it today, but somehow it was misplaced and lost. I think it got mixed in with some clothes that were taken to the Goodwill. I like to imagine it's under some little fella's pillow tonight—but then I have an imagination as wild as my throwing arm.

Sometimes the wisest investment of time is to put down the paper and pick up your ball glove or get out your bike. Maybe years from now your child will drive down your street and her heart will be flooded with sweet memories of times you spent together.

Chapter 42
MY YOUTHFUL FOLLY

It is amazing that my little brothers still speak to me at all. When they were small I tormented them without mercy. That's just the way I treated people I loved when I was a kid. At the time it was hard for them to understand the twisted psychology of that. I would tell you the details but then you probably wouldn't like me anymore—so I'll just keep most of them to myself and give you one representative example here.

Years ago on a summer day I spent the day with my dad, who was helping build a house on his break from teaching school. It was a long, hot day, so on the way home we stopped for a cold soft drink. I chose Seven-Up, which at the time was sold only in those wonderful dark green glass bottles. I finished it off quickly on the way home.

Walking through the kitchen I noticed some old dishwater standing in the sink and had an evil thought. Maybe you really can't help it when evil ideas pop into your mind, but you don't have to act on them. I did.

I laid my empty bottle down in the water and filled it about a third full of the water from the sink. With a sinister chuckle I toweled the outside of the bottle dry." Perfect," I thought. I went looking for my five-year-old brother, Kevin.

"Hey, Kevin, you want the rest of my pop?"

He came over to me eagerly. I remember the trusting look in his big innocent eyes. He was wearing overalls. He should have been bright enough to know something was up, but there he stood like a deer in the crosshairs.

"Sure," he said with an eager smile, and he grabbed the bottle with both hands and guzzled down a good gulp before he knew what he was doing.

Suddenly he let out a desperate wail and began to bound around the room clutching his neck. Instantly the whole family was in the room.

"What happened?" my dad demanded, for some reason looking directly at me.

"I gave him some old water from the sink. I was just kidding. It was a joke."

My sister said, "That wasn't water. I was soaking rags. That was bleach."

Immediately my dad snatched my little brother up and tried to induce vomiting. He sent me to the drug store for milk of magnesia to aid in the process. (Later he discovered this was the wrong way to treat ingestion of a small amount of bleach because it burns your throat coming back out again that way.) I rode like the wind, praying that my brother would not die, fighting back tears.

When I got home all was quiet. Kevin was still alive. He survived and grew into a strapping specimen of a man, served in the Marine Corps, married a fine wife, and they will soon have their eighth child. He pastors in northern Michigan. Miraculously he considers me his friend to this day, though he never has been quite as trusting as he used to be.

The whole thing is just a shameful memory to me now. If you are sometimes haunted by shameful memories from the past I commend to you an understanding of Christian theology. Meditation on the sins of your youth can be like drinking bleach. An understanding of the grace of forgiveness God offers freely through Christ Jesus his Son is like a long cold drink of sweet, sweet water on a hot day.

As you can imagine, with a past like mine, I have a great appreciation for the grace of God and forgiving brothers. I fully understand how David the Psalmist must have felt when he wrote, "Remember not the sins of my youth."

Chapter 43
MERCY

God has given me four sons and four daughters who are very careful not to hurt my feelings. I'm glad, because as much as I love them, they could hurt me deeply if they tried. I try to be a big boy but I still have some growing up to do.

We have at least one child, though, who is especially merciful. She is Holly, our eighteen-year-old. We think she has the gift of mercy described in the twelfth chapter of Paul's letter to the Romans. You don't really know what you are missing if you don't have a mercy-shower in your house. Our mercy-shower's gift showed up early.

She was about three and her mom was sad. In fact, she was crying. I'm not going into what made her cry because it would make me look bad.

She was sitting on the floor because all of our furniture was in the moving van and we were about to leave on a long journey to a faraway place to start a new phase of our lives. Our little mercy-shower, face wrinkled with concern, eyes dark and searching, walked over and put her hand on her mother's shoulder. She leaned over and peered straight into her eyes and said, "Mommy, you have feelings on your face."

When you have feelings on your face and an ache in your heart, it is good to have someone gifted with mercy around to hurt with you. I hope you have someone like Holly in your life.

.

Chapter 44
WHEN LIFE HURTS

A few years ago I took Wesley to the dentist. The dentist was a neighbor, a friend, a fine man, and a real pro. Wes was about five at the time and he looked exactly like I did at the same age.

Here's an idea for entertainment when you get tired of the Muzak in the dentist's office or when you weary of paging through the old magazines. Take note of the euphemisms a dentist uses for the unspeakable horrors he is about to perpetrate on the innocent children who are lured into his chambers.

A dentist never says, "I'm going to strap you down now, crush your tooth, and rip it out by the roots." What he says sounds something like this: "Hi there, little buddy. Hop up here in the chair and we are going to tug on that tooth a little and help it out of there." He says it all happy, like he is planning a trip to Disneyland.

The dentist gave Wes a series of instructions that I was quite sure he would not be able to remember." Here is what we are going to do. We are going to give you something to keep it from hurting too bad. You will feel a little pinch at first then maybe some pressure. You shouldn't feel pain though, just a little pressure. If you do feel pain you won't be able to say anything because we will have some things in your mouth, so if you do feel pain you don't have to say anything, just raise your hand. Do you understand?" The dentist took his right hand and raised it up. "Like this, okay?"

Wes looked up at the dentist with big trusting eyes and nodded. Then we plunged into conversation while he and his assistants worked on Wes. He worked and we talked for ten or fifteen minutes and Wes lay patiently in the chair. I admired the dentist for his ability to carry on a lively conversation while at the same time doing such complicated and important work. Well into our lively conversation I noticed movement. Little Wes lying perfectly still on the table was lifting his little hand in the air. I had forgotten the dentist's instruction about what to do if he felt pain, but Wes remembered. His hand was up and my heart went out to him. The dentist noticed it, but I reminded him to make sure. "Uh, Doc. Look, his hand is up. He raised his hand. He is feeling pain. It hurts," I said.

"I see that. We've got it," he calmly assured me. A picture of my little blonde Wes lying still on that table with his little hand in the air is forever fixed in my mind. I know I can't always shelter Wes from pain in this life, but when his little hand goes up I want to be there to do what I can.

Our Heavenly Father never promised us a life without pain, or cavities for that matter, but He has faithfully instructed us about what to do when life hurts. When life hurts, the Father notices and cares. Don't ever doubt it; just lift your hand and the heart of the Father will leap up and he will see your pain and come to your aid.

Chapter 45
AT THE END OF THE PARADE

Some people find it impossible to enjoy the moment because they are obsessed with the past or preoccupied with the future. That is not true about me. I am blessed with the ability to fully live in the moment.

This came into play last year on the final day of the National Baby Food Festival. It was the day of the Grand Parade. The parade came at the end of a weeklong festival in which our oldest daughter Holly was named the Festival Queen. I was given the honor of driving the float bearing the Queen's court. The parade went right down a major street in the town where we had lived and pastored for the past six years.

It was a perfect Saturday morning, sunny and cool. Holly sat on the Queen's throne. Her court rode with her. It was a very, very happy day for Holly and for each of us. I adjusted the rearview mirrors so I could watch my daughter's face while we drove the parade route. All along the way were friends and family members, each celebrating with us and shouting congratulations to Holly and taking pictures. "There's Holly. Hi, Holly!" Holly smiled and waved back, radiant. Her beautiful brown eyes glistened with joy, just like her mother's.

In front of us were a marching band and two convertibles, one bearing the Prince and the other the Princess of the festival. In what seemed like moments, we reached the east end of the street and the parade was over. I wanted to loop around the parade route again.

The parade ended on the east end of the street and took a sharp turn to the south. When we turned the corner the marching band had dissipated. The two convertibles ahead of us disappeared. I didn't notice where they went. The parade entries behind kept coming, and for the first time all day it occurred to me that I did not know where to go. I vaguely remembered that they had given me a sheet of paper the night before with instructions, but in the confusion and celebration I had misplaced it. I had been living in the moment through the whole parade, but now I had no idea where to go or what to do with the float or where to deposit my cargo of young beauties.

I couldn't stop; the whole parade was behind me. The street ahead was barricaded. I couldn't turn to the east because I would have to pull the float with a load of beauty queens into traffic on the main highway. It seemed that everyone watched me with amusement but no one offered any help. I had been living in the moment through the whole parade without a single thought about what I would do at the end.

Finally I asked the young ladies to get off the float while I pulled out onto the main road to turn around. They waited in their formal dresses on the street corner while I got the whole rig safely turned around. Eventually I was able to return the float to the origin of the parade and the young ladies rejoined their families.

I am glad that I have the ability to fully enjoy the moment without being burdened by the past or worried about the future, but I chastised myself for not planning ahead. The only thing injured was my ego, but it made me think. Such is life for most people. It is a parade, perhaps pleasant enough, but it is over much faster than we expect and many have made no concrete plans for the end. Living in the moment is good, but not making concrete plans for eternity is tragic.

Live while you live and milk all the joy available from every day but take time to do some quiet thinking about ultimate things. Where do you stand with God? Where will you spend eternity? Where will you go when life comes to an end? *Carpe Diem* . . . seize the day, but remember to think eternity. Be sure you know where you are going when the parade of life comes to an end.

Chapter 46
OPPORTUNITIES IN DISGUISE

One morning this week I woke up with ideas running through my head that I had to get on my hard drive. I was speaking at a conference. I jumped up, opened my laptop, and began to write as the sun came up over the mountains. I was in Tennessee, feasting my eyes on the beautiful green hills. The week was cool. Breeze blew soft and steady through the window just like I like it. After a couple good hours of writing I began to think about how good a nice strong cup of coffee would go down just then. When I am writing and the ideas and phrases are coming freely, I hate to stop, because sometimes it takes days to get back to the same level of productivity.

I woke up Kyle and Chuck and asked if either of them was in the mood to get a dozen Krispy Kreme doughnuts for the family and a big stout coffee for me. Since we were in Tennessee, Chuck volunteered to go . . . maybe it was the spirit of theVolunteers that came over him. He grabbed the keys and left on his errand. I went back to my laptop.

In about a half-hour I began to be distracted thinking about how good that coffee would taste. About that time I heard Chuck come through the door and I shouted, "Do you have my coffee, Chuck?"

"I did, Dad, but I dropped it in the parking lot."

I got up. "Did it all spill out?" I asked, hoping for just a drink of the coffee I had so anticipated.

"It all spilled out."

I fought a deep frustration within and considered leaving to get more. When I checked my watch I realized I would have only enough time to groom and dress and get to the morning session. Chuck said, "I'm sorry, Dad. I kept it from spilling in the van all the way here and it hit a mirror on the car parked beside me in the parking lot." He had a frustrated look on his face. I felt bad for him. I noticed he watched my reaction closely. I had really been looking forward to drinking that coffee . . . but when I thought about it, it really was humorous. I laughed and said, "Don't worry about it, Chuck. I guess I was supposed to go without my coffee today."

When he saw my reaction, the dark frustration left his face and it was replaced with the smile that makes him so fun to be around.

Within an hour I was sitting in the morning session listening to Gary Smalley, and it hit me that God had blessed me in a special way that morning. There is not a day that passes that I don't try to think of ways to express my love to each of the children. I have often thought of ways to show Chuck that I love him in a special way. The

Lord knows that is a great desire in my heart. And early that morning he arranged a special circumstance for me to demonstrate to Chuck that I love him with all my heart, and all it cost me was a cup of coffee. A good deal if you ask me. Be careful you don't overlook the special opportunities the Lord arranges for you to love people. They are easy to miss. Here's a thought for the day: "Irritations are opportunities in disguise."

Well, I'd like to go on, but I think I'll go brew a pot of coffee.

Chapter 47
FREDDIE, WHO WAS DUMB

We once had a dog we called Freddie. I can't remember why we gave him that name . . . In fact, Freddie wasn't a him at all. Come to think of it, Freddie was adopted from some neighbors who moved away. She looked a little like a squat German shepherd.

Freddie wasn't the sharpest knife in the drawer. She was affectionate but lacking in intelligence. The most vivid example of Freddie's ignorance occurred one winter day when we were celebrating a heavy snowfall. As the snow thickened the children were jubilant. We lived at the base of a steep hill and we were waiting for the first snow heavy enough to cover the stubble on the hill so we could try out an old toboggan we had found stored in an outbuilding. It was a fine old wooden toboggan. When I see things like that I wish they could empty out their memory to me in speech.

At lunch, over grilled cheese and tomato soup, I tendered my plan to the children. They all shouted with delight. Leaving their lunch half-eaten, they began to pull on sweaters and sweatshirts and coats and mittens and caps. We went out to the shed and brought forth the wonderful old toboggan. It was wooden and weathered. It may have been an antique. We pulled it to the very top of the hill. I stood in front of the toboggan to keep it from taking off prematurely and began to give direction to each of the children . . . I got on last, right up front, and put Heidi in my lap for the ride. The moment I lifted my legs and put them in the toboggan it shot off down the hill. It immediately occurred to me—for the first time—that there was no way to steer a toboggan and there was no way to slow it down.

The snow was flying up in our faces and we were going lots faster than we planned to go. There was no way to steer or stop or slow the huge sled now. My life flashed before my eyes.

I wondered if Lois would be able to find the life insurance papers. I wondered if my body would be recognizable after the crash.

Suddenly straight ahead of us was our dog Freddie—the Dumb One. Freddie just didn't plan to move. She never did, not one inch in either direction. She just stood there and stared blankly at us. Unable to avoid her we ran right over the top of her.

Running over Freddie didn't even slow us down. We were still careening wildly down the hill. For the first time that day I began to think ahead. There was a ditch at the bottom of the hill. I wondered if we could ramp the ditch and how fast we would still be going as we approached a huge pine in front of the house. Ramp the ditch we did in a second, picking up speed. We were headed for the tree. I shouted "bail out" just before the toboggan hit the tree. We all leaned off the sled and buried ourselves in snow. We were shaken but unhurt.

When we stood up and began dusting off snow we discovered that Heidi's face was covered with snow, her eyes frozen shut. I looked around and Freddie came walking up, looking curious and unharmed. We took a quick vote and decided by consensus to go inside and drink hot cocoa by the fire for a while. Maybe we could forget what had just happened.

We put the toboggan away for another day and made a mental note to have Freddie's IQ checked before we let her out in public again. We were all pretty sure she was too dumb to be allowed to roam around without supervision.

The sad fact is we are all vulnerable to areas of ignorance or lapses of good sense. Like when I put the whole family on the toboggan or like when Freddie didn't have the good sense to get out of the way. There is a proverb about that . . . it has to do with people that are just too stupid. I'm glad God makes allowances for stupid people.

So here is a bit of advice to you from a guy who has been up and down the hill a few times. Before you get your whole family on a toboggan, you might want to figure out how to steer and stop first. And you might want to put away your dumb dog so you don't run over him.

Chapter 48
KEEPING THE PICTURE IN FOCUS

When Bud and Charlotte were young, there was something missing in their lives and they didn't know what it was. They sometimes left their three small children alone at night and went out dancing and drinking. Eventually they separated and then divorced. Charlotte had a man friend.

It was around that time someone invited the girls to Vacation Bible School, where they were introduced to Christ. Then Charlotte attended the funeral of a neighbor, where she heard the Gospel message. She began to attend her neighbor's church and later discovered that the neighbor named Mrs. Rice had been praying for her and for her children. Their names were written on a prayer list and kept in her Bible.

Soon Bud and Charlotte were a family again. Altogether they would be married fifty years, not counting their time of separation. They raised their three children for the Lord and they even adopted another child. Then there were two girls and two boys.

Bud developed a hunger for the Bible and Christian books. Somewhere he found a weekly periodical called *The Sword of the Lord*. The editor of *The Sword of the Lord*, an evangelist named John R. Rice, wrote a book titled *The Christian Home*. Bud read the book and kept a copy of it handy all the time.

Bud was not quick to discipline his children. He did not like to punish them. He was a man of few words. He did not lecture them. When his children argued or things weren't as they should be in the home, he would sit them all down and read long passages from Rice's book on the home.

Years later his daughter would say she dreaded those times and would rather have been grounded or disciplined in some other way. She often mentioned this in the years to come and her siblings would all groan at the memory. I heard the story many times myself, because Bud was my grandfather.

Years ago, before we banished television from our home, we owned an old TV set that a friend had given us. Sometimes the picture would get fuzzy, like you were watching without glasses. I noticed a reset button on the back of the set. When you pushed the reset button the picture would become clear again.

Last week I was frustrated with my children because they were being argumentative and making trouble. When that happens I am often grieved and frustrated. I feel like somehow I am failing as a dad. I feel like we are losing our focus. I want to find the reset button and bring the vision for a harmonious, loving Christian family back into focus again. Times like this often drive me to my knees. I try to think of ways to recast the original vision for a family marked by godliness. Frankly I fear what can happen if we begin to wander from the commandments of God and the principles of godly living.

I was sitting in a restaurant when it hit me that that must have been what my grandfather was doing when he gathered his children and read to them long passages from Dr. Rice's book. He remembered the emptiness and guilt and pain of a broken family. He remembered the hurt of separation and the guilt of sin and he didn't ever want to go back. He wanted something better for his own children than what his sinful past had given him. My grandfather was searching for some way to remind himself and his family about what they believed and held dear.

That may be the most important thing a godly man can do: continually keep a picture of a godly, spiritually healthy family before his wife and sons and daughters. As long as there is breath in my body, no matter how hard it is, I am going to keep hitting the reset button to keep a picture of a godly, happy, holy, healthy family in focus in our hearts. Pray for me. We need it. We all always will.

Chapter 49
THICK OR THIN

Last night Hope said, "Dad, even if you were fat I would still love you and I would still hug you and snuggle with you."

When Kyle was a little boy he rode a school bus for one school year. In the morning I always brewed a pot of coffee, and I would walk him out to the road where we would wait for the school bus. I always hated seeing the little guy in his neat school clothes and mother-attended hair climb up the steps into the big yellow diesel dragon and drive away. I would stand and watch until the bus drove over the hill and out of sight and then walk slowly back into the house.

When the bus returned in the afternoon I tried to be there to meet him with a basketball, or a baseball and glove, or a football. Skipper, our white golden retriever, would be with me. We would play. Kyle is a married man now, but then he was just a small boy.

One day he got off the bus and said, "Hi, Dad. When the other kids on the bus say, 'Your dad is fat,' I say, 'He is not, he's just right. ' " As you can imagine, I had mixed feelings about that comment.

It is nice to have someone who is willing to defend you, even in the face of obvious evidence against you. That's the kind of loyalty that warms your heart years later when you still brew coffee but you drink it alone and your little buddy no longer sleeps in the next room or tosses a football with you on a late-fall afternoon.

I talk to a lot of people about being fat. It hurts. Being fat, it is easy to believe that people would love you more if you could just somehow be slender. It's even hard not to believe that God would like you more if you were slim. But satisfaction in God and freedom from the bondage of gluttony require a deep, settled satisfaction in your soul that God loves you already and longs to be your satisfaction.

Chapter 50
TALKING IN THE NIGHT

Years ago in my room at Moody I would pray at night with my roommate Paul Davidheizer. We would get in our beds and turn off the light; then we would each pray. After we prayed we would usually talk for a while. Often I would still be talking after I discovered that Paul was asleep. He was a great guy but I could just talk longer than he could listen.

I am almost always the first one up in the morning around our place. When bedtime comes for me, Hope, who is four and enjoys the luxury of sleeping in, usually has another good half-hour of energy left in her day. She doesn't wind down slowly at the end of the day. She finishes her day like a runner straining for the tape. She always has a little burst, a little sprint to the finish. I know in a perfect world parents put their children to sleep at night. That's not always the way it works at our house.

The other night I was exhausted and eager to sleep. I had to get an early start the next day and a long "to do" list waiting for me. I got into bed. But Hope was in no mood to sleep. She had a bed of her own, but she came in our room and jumped in bed with us and refused to lie down. For a few minutes she used the bed for a trampoline until I made her stop.

"Lie down right now and go to sleep, Hope," I warned her, and I turned off the light.

She lay down but my warning and the darkness had no effect on her whatsoever. She jabbered on about her day, her dolls, her diet, and her general philosophy of life, unabated. She punctuated her stories with pointed questions that demanded a response. One of us would mumble a barely coherent answer and she would chatter on.

Finally she interrupted her own energetic soliloquy with a question:"Am I talking too much?"

With that we were both awake and chuckling. We both quickly assured her that she was not at all talking too much. When heavy eyes ended my day she still had stories to tell.

As I drifted off to sleep I took comfort in the thought of my unsleeping Heavenly Father who never tires of hearing me talk. He wants to know when I have something to celebrate. He likes it when I tell him my fears and unburden my guilty heart to him. He listens when I chatter excitedly about my plans. He cares about what I think. He even stays awake at night and listens when I am talking in the dark. He can listen longer than I can talk.

Chapter 51
CATASTROPHE IN THE BATHROOM

When I was a boy I got into a lot of mischief. I like that word: mischief. It has an innocent sound to it. Sometimes I got in trouble for the mischief I did. Sometimes I didn't get caught. Other times I got in trouble for things I didn't do. Sometimes I was blamed for things over which I had no control. Some days my life just took an ugly turn and one bad thing led to another, like falling dominoes.

One afternoon I was sitting on the toilet after school in the privacy of our own bathroom. I finished my business and rose to leave. I looked up and there conveniently in front of me were two handles for the metal wardrobe in which my mother stored cleaning supplies and clean linens and towels.

When I pulled myself up, the door came open and the cabinet started to tip over. I didn't have time to pull my pants up. With my pants around my ankles I pushed the cabinet back into an upright position. Then I bent to pull my pants up. What I didn't know was that the cabinet was resting on the base molding, and when I let go to pull up my pants the cabinet door opened and the wardrobe started down again. This time things began to spill out and crash into the toilet.

My sister Melony heard the commotion and took it upon herself to whip open the door, whereupon she began to scream loudly. She didn't come in and help. She didn't go out and shut the door. She just stood there and screamed while I struggled with my pants around my ankles to get the cabinet back into an upright position and dodge the cans and jars and linens that were falling into the toilet.

This was forty years ago, but what is fresh in my mind is the thing that bothered me most— not the mayhem in the bathroom but my irritation with my sister for standing there screaming while my pants were down. I try not to be bitter, but when I think of that to this day it troubles me. How could she do that to me knowing that if I bent to pull up my pants the cabinet would fall over, and if I didn't I would be exposed and publicly shamed? That's a heavy burden to carry for four decades.

My mom was talking on the phone. I could have told her that once the kids are home trying to talk on the phone is probably not a good idea, but since I was only five she wouldn't have listened. Mom came in and saw the toilet full of towels, linens, broken furniture polish, and other things.

The first thing she said was, "Kenny, pull your pants up!"

I tried to tell her that for the last five minutes pulling my pants up was my one objective in life but she didn't want to listen. She just turned and said, "Get out of my sight." I did. I have been trying to stay out of sight as much as possible since.

The other day my mom and I were having a laugh about this incident. It's good to remember that when everything is coming unraveled in your life and no matter how hard you try you can't get your life together, and when all the bad things you have ever done are catching up to you at once, that one day you will be able to laugh about it. Trust me, you will. You will laugh some day. In the meantime it might be a good idea to get in the habit of locking the bathroom door when you use it.

Chapter 52
ATTENTION, PLEASE!

Kids have always misbehaved. They always will. It's like a sport for adults to try to figure that out. As hard as it is to imagine, even I sometimes misbehaved in my wayward youth. A generation ago they labeled this "depravity." In a more enlightened age, we began to call it "juvenile delinquency." That had social overtones.

After a while they gave this a clinical-sounding name that made it sound like a medical condition. They started calling it "hyperactivity." About that time they even started treating it with medication. Since then it has become a growth industry.

Recently the name for misbehavior was changed to "attention deficit." I like that, although I've never been real excited about calling a need for attention a disorder. That makes it seem like you have a bad twitch or something. But "attention deficit," that has a nice ring to it. When I was little they used to say, "Kenny needs attention."

Well, that was then and this is now and guess what? The other night I was longing to spend some time with my wife, just being with her talking or sitting quietly in the same room. Sometimes I just want her all to myself and I want her complete and undivided attention. It occurred to me that Kenny is all grown up now and Kenny still needs attention. I don't need medication. I don't need therapy. I don't need ink blots. I don't need behavioral modification. But when I'm around Lois and the children sometimes I still like attention and I'm not ashamed of it.

I may have stumbled across one of the great secrets of the universe here; little boys need a lot of attention. Big boys still need a lot of attention. And though it is an untested hypothesis, I am toying with the theory that girls need attention too. I may be on to something here. I think there is something powerful about having someone's undivided attention.

If you have a child that is misbehaving, try giving him a little attention. If your husband is a little annoying, pay attention to him. See what happens. Let me know if it works. Maybe I will write a book about it and make a lot of money and do TV and radio interviews and get a lot of attention.

Chapter 53
LONGING FOR THE BLESSING

We all long for the verbal blessing of others. This longing starts early and continues all through our lives. Last night we were all lying in our bunks in the cabin. The children were getting in their last squirms and giggles. When things were finally quiet I could hear Hope talking to Mom.

"Mom, when are you going to teach me to cook?"

"Why do you want to learn to cook, Hope?"

"When I get married I need to know how to cook."

Hope is five so I was a little surprised to find that she was already thinking about honing her homemaking skills.

Lois asked her, "Hope, what do you want to learn to make?"

Without hesitation she said, "I want to know how to make pies."

I think Hope is going to make her husband very happy some day. Men appreciate women who take pie-making seriously.

The room fell silent for a moment and then Hope began to making sneezing sounds. She wasn't really sneezing, she was pretending to sneeze. She "sneezed" three or four times and then she was quiet for a while. Finally she said with disgust, "Isn't anybody going to bless me?"

Quickly out of the darkness voices came. All of Hope's brothers and sisters and her mom and dad chimed in together to give her the blessing she asked for.

"Bless you, Hope. Bless you," everyone said. They were the last words of the day. People all around us every day wherever we go long for the blessing of others. Often when they come to the end of the day and lie in the darkness with their thoughts they have to go to sleep night after night without it. We should be quick to bless others even before they ask for it. And we should all know someone who loves us and takes pie-making seriously. Life would be a lot happier then, now wouldn't it?

Chapter 54
GUMMY BEAR ATTACK

I noticed one day—I suppose my children pointed it out to me—a special quality that gummy bears have. If you lick them and throw them they will stick to almost anything. If you lick them and throw them you can stick them to the ceiling. You can throw them at a car and they will stick to the car. We discovered this one day out in traffic. I was sitting at the traffic light and I noticed an attractive woman pulled up behind me. I had a little difficulty keeping from noticing her. She was very attractive and I had the distinct feeling that she noticed me. In fact I'm sure she was looking steadily at me.

Immediately a thought came to my mind. I thought, "It would sure be fun to jump out of the car and do something memorable." That is when I remembered the special qualities of a gummy bear. I just happened to have a generous supply of them. I grabbed a handful of gummy bears and jumped out of the car. I ran back to the car behind me and quickly fired four or five gummies into her windshield. To my shock I saw something in my peripheral vision. My sons had also jumped from the car armed with their own gummies and they fired away at the pretty woman's car too.

We jumped back into the car and sped away, leaving the pretty woman stunned and motionless behind the wheel. The boys thought it was great fun but later at home when I ran into their mother she let me know immediately that she had not been amused. She said most of all when we all jumped out of the car and threw gummy bears at her car she was just embarrassed for us.

It's not as easy as it used to be to impress a beautiful woman and gain her admiration. When you try, sometimes she is just amused and not impressed. Sometimes she is filled with pity— not the respect you hoped to gain. Sometimes instead of admiring you she's just embarrassed for you.

Recently I was speaking at a homeschool conference. I told the gummy bear story and I got a big laugh from all the people. After my talk I forgot all about it. But my audience remembered—three of the young people in particular. They happened to know where I live and where I keep my car. This became very obvious the next day. My cell phone rang. It was my son, Chuck.

"Dad, have you seen your Volvo today?" "No, what's wrong." "You have to come and see it yourself.

Someone has plastered it with at least three hundred gummy bears."

I laughed and mourned my foolishness. It was as if I had given a group of pyromaniacs instructions about how to make bombs. It reminded me of the rogues in Australia who strapped a stick of dynamite to a kangaroo just to see what would happen. They lit the fuse and stood back in a special depth of ignorance induced by drunkenness to enjoy the show. The funny part is that they ended up having to walk all the way back to town because the frightened animal sought refuge under their truck.

I was reminded again that I have to be careful about what I say, because words have a way of coming back to trouble me. The Bible says, *"Death and life are in the power of the tongue, and those who love it will eat its fruit" (Proverbs 18:21)*. Sometimes my words are life-giving, but it is possible for them to get me into a real mess. A real mess.

Chapter 55
TOP-HEAVY

Chuck, our third-born child, second-born son, is a grown man now. When he was small he was especially top-heavy. He had a big head when he was a little kid and it has taken him years for his body to catch up to his head. He was really a cute kid but he was as tipsy as a weeble toy, so top-heavy he just couldn't stay on his feet.

Once he was standing in a safety seat that was on the floor of the garage and he leaned over the back of the seat until it tipped over. His forehead smacked on the cement floor of the garage, raising a big knot on his head.

When he was very small he jumped off the kitchen counter one Sunday morning. He recovered from the fall without any need for medical attention. A few weeks later he tumbled down a flight of stairs into the basement in a walker. Other than his being a little slow it didn't seem to have any effect on him.

One of his funniest tumbles was after a little feast at Taco Bell. We were walking to the car. Chuck's little arms were inside his shirt because the air conditioning had been too cold in the restaurant. He tripped on the sidewalk and went down like a sack of potatoes. With his arms in his shirt he had no way to catch himself, so he just tucked one shoulder and rolled on impact. He wasn't hurt but we laughed so hard it hurt our sides. Again, other than the original mild brain damage, he seemed unaffected by his fall.

I was late for church one Wednesday night and took off before I made sure little Chuck was safely belted in. He was standing up in the "way back" of the station wagon. When I turned the corner and accelerated onto the highway, he went crashing around the back of the car. It struck me as funny and I couldn't stop laughing, but Lois was not even mildly amused.

Three times he had to be sown up after a fall. Once when he was chasing a ball he fell against a door and opened a gash in his forehead you don't want me to describe. (Chuck's first word was ball and every time he saw one he went into gyrations. He was happy to risk injury to get one. When he played shortstop in Little League he would wait on a slow grounder so he could dive and backhand it like Brooks Robinson.)

Another time he was just a little shaver and we were walking through the grocery store. He heard that we were going to buy popsicles. In his enthusiasm he whirled around and ran straight into the shopping cart with his face. That one required needlework too.

About three years ago he was riding a bike on a half-pipe at a skate park. His bike malfunctioned (imagine) and he came crashing down on—you guessed it—his face.

Have you noticed a pattern here? One thing you can say for Chuck: He may fall but he will land on his face.

About a year ago, before Chuck had turned eighteen, he decided he would like to try to knock down some college credit working here in the Verity program. He was younger than all the students but he gave it a try. I told him if he passed I would buy him a latte at Starbucks to celebrate.

When he took his first test, though, he failed by a few points. He was discouraged and I could tell he was struggling with defeat. I was a little afraid we had made a mistake encouraging him to start so soon. When he told me he failed he was so dejected. I said, "Chuck, hop in the car. We're going to Starbucks to celebrate."

"To celebrate what, Dad?"

"Chuck," I said, "we are going to Starbucks to celebrate your amazing potential. You can do this. You are just going to have to give it more than you have. It's not going to be easy. You know they don't just give away credible college degrees."

So to Starbucks we went and we celebrated his amazing potential in faith. And then he came home and stalled for a few months, probably afraid to try again, but in February he took another test and he passed. After that there was no looking back. He took a break to serve for a summer at camp, traveled on a missions trip to Mexico, and now he is just one class from completing his degree. He did the four-year degree in about two years. Not bad for a kid who lands on his head regularly is it?

Chapter 56
LONG-AGO AND FARAWAY THOUGHTS

Sometimes I get to thinking long-ago and faraway thoughts. Sometimes long-ago and faraway thoughts make me smile. Sometimes long-ago and faraway thoughts make me cry. But some of my favorite long-ago and faraway thoughts make my mouth water.

I was on a long fast one day when I had a long-ago and faraway thought that made me laugh and cry and it made my mouth water. The faraway part was in the countryside near a charming little village called Charm, nestled in a place they call Doughty Valley in Holmes County, Ohio.

Since Holmes County is remote, everything in Holmes County is remote. Charm is a remote village in a remote county and the place that makes me smile and cry and makes my mouth water is not even in Charm. You can't even see it from there. It is off a side road of a side road.

It's a bakery run by an Amish woman named Mary. They call it "Mary's Bakery." (The Amish folks are great cooks and bakers and impressively enterprising, but they are just not all that creative when it comes to naming things.) Anyway, I've been making my way to Mary's Bakery for years. Usually I stop to get a cup of real coffee to take with me, because whatever it is Mary serves is not coffee. Then I walk into Mary's gaslit bakery and I go over and stand in front of the huge glass bakery case. It is filled with a variety of cheese tarts. There are raspberry, cherry, lemon, blackberry, and plain cheese tarts, and they are good enough to put a smile on your face, bring a tear to your eye, and make your mouth water all at the same time from miles and miles and years and years away.

If something is good enough, it can make you smile, put a tear in your eye, and maybe even make your mouth water from many, many miles away and maybe even many, many years away. Something that good calls you across many miles and back over many years, back and back again. That should be our goal in our homes. It is by our daily efforts and by the exercise of Christlike love that we gather our sons and daughters and others we cherish around the fire of real Christian life.

Genuine faith lived out in daily family life should be a very, very winsome thing. Our conversation and our courtesies, our patient listening and our gentle words should be like the fragrance of supper on the stove that draws our children in from riding their bikes to the supper table.

Then maybe one day when our children are miles and miles or years and years away, they will still have the memory of the fragrance of our faith. Maybe the voice of that faith will call them back and back again to the faith of their fathers. Maybe it will make them smile and cry and make their mouth water for more.

Chapter 57
A GENTLE PLACE TO FALL

One year during apple blossom and flowering Dogwood time I glanced out the window to see my neighbor Dave conducting a sacred rite of passage. He was teaching his little girl to ride her bike without training wheels. I got a lump in my throat at the sweetness of the memory of teaching my three older daughters to ride their bikes. I have only one left to teach; after that it will be my granddaughters by God's good grace.

Dave was teaching his daughter to ride her bike out in the street. Not a bad idea but not the best plan either. I am a man of great experience and no small success at this matter of teaching daughters to ride their bikes without training wheels.

Here's the way I do it. First I take off the training wheels, then I position the little bike at the top of a gentle slope in the lawn. I make sure the grass is high enough to provide a little cushion for the inevitable fall. Then I give the bike the slightest little push. Usually your little girl will pedal for a while as she learns to balance herself. When she starts to lose momentum she will usually tip over, but she will be going slowly enough that she can often just step off her bike, or if she falls it will be a tumble into soft, fragrant green grass.

At first I chase behind her and I am there to pick her up and laugh with her when she falls. Later I will stand at the top of the slope and holler, "Great job. Let's do it again and we'll get Mom. She won't believe what you can do." Or you can shout, "Wow, that was great! Do it again and we'll call Grandma. I can't believe how fast you are learning to do that!"

When she makes any positive progress it is very important that you cheer like she just debuted at Carnegie Hall.

When I close my eyes I can smell the sweetness of springtime. I can hear my daughter's happy laughter. I can see her hair blowing in the wind. And I want to go back, but I can't. She's asking for the keys to the car so she can go to the mall.

Chapter 58
TAKE IN THE VIEW

When I was about fourteen we took a family vacation through the Great Smoky Mountains National Park. When you drive through the Smokies there are winding roads all through the mountains. It is, in places, beautiful beyond description. I mean to return someday and share the beauty with my family.

Along the way there are places to pull off to enjoy the view. The pull-outs are lined with low walls constructed from native stone. I think many of them were the work of the Civilian Conservation Corps. They are a quiet and valuable attraction, beautiful and understated. There is no admission charge to enjoy them. They would be easy to miss.

You could go whizzing past to get to the nearest trinket shop filled with things made many oceans and continents distant but that would be a mistake. The kinds of things they sell at those shops are made cheap and quick somewhere else and stamped with the name of the nearest attraction. They are not mountain crafts created by local artists who have the hills in their own hearts. They are just cheap trinkets. They won't last and they won't satisfy.

The mountains, the valleys, the wild birds, the wildlife, the wildflowers, the native timber— they are real. The beauty of the mountains is there for the taking, free of charge, the bounty of rich and poor, wise and simple. Just to stand there and take in the autumn color is the kind of thing that will still hang in your memory many decades from now, like the mist over the mountains in the early morning. The beauty and order of creation will never be out of style.

In this journey we call "living" there are beautiful things to see and there are places along the way to pull over quietly. I don't want to be the kind of person who is obsessed with gathering things that I cannot keep, when there are beauties and wonders all around me. When I am long gone and my children and grandchildren think of me I want them to remember me as the kind of guy that pulled over and took in the scenery whenever possible. I want them to know that I saw beauty in each of them. I want them to learn from watching me how to see the hand of God in all the world around them.

Along the path of living maybe they will say, "Dad would have pulled off to take in the scenery here. Do you remember how Grandpa's eyes would cloud with tears at a sight like this?"

Chapter 59
SUNSET ON SUMMER

Things are changing fast. I am sailing away at a clip from my youth into uncharted waters they call "midlife." I am finding it bittersweet. I used to have so many plans. I still do. But now along with the plans I have memories like treasured photos of children who have grown up or places that have grown sacred.

One memory that will never fade from my mind took place on Labor Day our last year all together under one roof as a family. The next summer our firstborn son Kyle would leave for a year of missionary service and then it would be off to college a continent away.

We had spent the day together in the yard working in the herb garden, grilling out, reading, talking, and sipping lemonade. We played a little touch football, Mom standing guard with a water hose to make sure no one trespassed into her flower beds. Toward evening we all agreed to drive to Grand Haven and watch the sun set on Lake Michigan.

In a resort town like Grand Haven the whole atmosphere changes after Labor Day. When we arrived it was cool and fall-like. The sun was falling steadily into the lake. We strode quickly, trying to reach the lighthouse before the sun disappeared. As we walked the sun touched the horizon and then steadily sank from sight.

As we were walking along, more than once I heard someone say, "That was over so fast." Everyone had gathered and waited to see the last sunset of summer and they were talking about how quickly the sun had set. All I could think about, walking out toward the sunset with my precious firstborn son, was about how quickly the sunset on summer had come.

The whole family gathered at the foot of the lighthouse on the end of the pier and watched the sky turn golden orange. A few boats growled into the harbor for the evening. A ship sat out on the horizon moving imperceptibly slow, going who knows where. Gentle waves lapped the rocks. Occasionally a bigger wave spouted up in spray and mist. The wind swept strong over the point and we all stood close to keep each other warm. There was a sweetness in the air. My heart grew tender and alive to the world around me.

My mind went back through the years with my son. They passed swift as a summer, short as a sunset. We went to a few ball games together. We camped out together a few times. Together we gazed into a few campfires. Together we floated a few rivers. We went fishing a few times. We washed the car together a few times. I taught him to tie a tie, shake hands, and drink his coffee black. I taught him the books of the Bible. I taught him to ride a bike and a few days later I taught him to drive. Together we laughed and cried. We loved a couple of dogs together, together we buried them, and together we hurt. Together we tried to understand the mysteries of life and love. A few times we walked together under a full moon in awe at the wonder of God's world. Together we sang and prayed and worshiped God. And soon, for the first time, we would go on— but not together. The reality of it settled in on me that night on the pier.

As the purple of night pushed in on the pale blue and orange twilight, we turned and made our way back. Kyle was holding his little sister Hope. She was giggling over his shoulder at her mother when suddenly she said "Momma" for the first time. Lois was delighted and her eyes glowed. Hope looked back with the same lively brown eyes. One child ready to go make his way in the world was carrying another just learning to talk.

When we reached the boardwalk we all turned and saw the lighthouse and pier lights blinking red against the dusk. A string of white harbor lights lined the catwalk. The afterglow of the sun cast the lighthouse and the pier light in a sharp black silhouette. Stars appeared in the growing darkness overhead. Lovers held one another or walked hand in hand. Fishermen packed up their gear and sauntered toward shore. Children climbed on the rocks. Everyone made toward shore along the lighted walkway.

In an hour we had watched the sun set on summer and turned toward autumn with a lifelong memory in our hearts. I felt the pain that always comes with love, and my soul whispered,

"Breathe deep, walk slow, hold tight to those you love, the sun is setting, and it will be over so fast."

Whenever I think back on that evening I hear these words again and again: "That was over so fast."

IMPORTANT ACKNOWLEDGMENTS

Without the Lord Jesus Christ I wouldn't have a family, I wouldn't have a life, I wouldn't have a clue. I would be without hope and without God in the world. My heart soars heavenward to thank Him continually every day of my life. He is so worthy. One day I want to bow before Him, bringing with me each of the children He has given me and the generations that follow them to worship Him at His Throne. He has inspired good things in some other people I want to thank, too:

I am especially grateful to Sam Allen. This book would not be in your hands without his interest and investment in my life.

Laura DeMasie (laura. graphicdesign@gmail.com) did the cover and the layout. It's better than I imagined and I have a really good imagination.

Donna and Timus Rees (editor_donna@rees.ws) not only were my cheerleaders, but Donna pored over every word of this book. I'm sure she has read it more than I have. The Reeses are the kind of family this book is about.

I am grateful to them and others for making these stories appealing and helping me get them into the hands of people.

ABOUT THE AUTHOR

For more information on
Ken Pierpont's writing and ministry go to:
KenPierpont.com